.

ROYAL AIR FORCE
MIDDLE EAST COMMAND

Dedication

I dedicated my book to all those members of His Majesty's Armed Forces who have made the ultimate sacrifice or have suffered or are suffering from physical and/or mental injuries in carrying out their Pledge of Allegiance both faithful and truly to the Crown. Also not forgetting their families and loved ones for the loss, pain and the distress they have suffered.

What is Parkinson's?

Parkinson's is a progressive degenerative neurological condition. It causes problems in the brain that gets worse over time. There is no known cure. People with Parkinson's don't have enough of the chemical dopamine in their brain because the nerve cells that produce it are dead or dying. The rate of loss differs from person to person. No two people are the same and their symptoms differ.

Around 145,000 people live with Parkinson's in the UK. Globally it is the fastest growing neurological condition.

Parkinsonism, is a term that covers several conditions, including Parkinson's and others with similar symptoms. Some, including healthcare professionals and people with the condition, call it Parkinson's disease or PD. It is not known exactly why people get Parkinson's. Researchers think it's a combination of age, genetic, and environmental factors that cause the dopamine-producing nerve cells to die. Without dopamine people can find their movement and thinking is affected and it takes longer to do things. Because it affects the muscles, there is nothing in your body that can't be affected, eating, breathing, speaking, bowels, bladder movement and thinking. Symptoms and progression differ from person to person. Trips and falls are risks.

I thank you for the purchase of my book. It will support research into this destructive and debilitating disease and is much appreciated.

Endorsements

Jane Asher is an English actor and has worked extensively in films and TV. She is also famous for her cakes and cake books. Jane was President of Parkinson's UK from February 2007 until 2023. During this time Jane was involved in launching campaigns to improve research into Parkinson's. Jane also visited and took part in the Swindon Parkinson's Branch Tai Chi Class. Following the class and over refreshments, Jane spent time talking to those with Parkinson's, their carers and our Tai Chi instructor Andy Wright at that time.

"If you'd told me I was going to enjoy reading a book about life on an RAF base over the course of a year I'd have found it hard to believe you... how wrong I would have been! And how lucky that I was such an admirer of Dave's through having got to know him during his magnificent chairmanship of the Swindon branch of Parkinson's UK, that when he sent me a draft to read I knew it would be well written and fascinating. What I didn't know was that it would also be both powerful and touching, dramatic and romantic, ranging from the horror of a terrifying massacre to the beautiful references to his much loved wife. It's a wonderful read, accompanied by plenty of contemporary photographs, and Dave has done a wonderful job.

I wish Dave and Daf many years of happiness ahead, and I thank him for introducing me to this terrific read. With my love and congratulations" – Jane Asher

"My good friend Dave Logan has written an engaging and entertaining account of life on an RAF base in Oman at a pivotal moment in British strategic military history. Arriving just after Wilson's "East of Suez" retreat from Aden, Dave found himself in a region where old powers were withdrawing, and new powers were rising, and the results are most interesting" – Yours ever Robert

The Rt Hon Sir Robert Buckland KBE KC MP

"Such an entertaining reminiscence. What I liked about it was the attention to little details: The triple bunks which meant that men in the top bunks had to avoid sitting up suddenly in case their heads encountered the ceiling fan; The fact that VC10s in military use had the seats facing the back; The flying tit.

I knew nothing about that part of the world but this book brought it to life and made it very personal with a good choice of photos." – Paul

Paul Mayhew-Archer MBE (Co-writer of 'The Vicar of Dibley' and Mrs Browns Boys). Paul is also a multi-award winning writer, script editor, radio producer, comedian and a dear friend.

As we entered the editing stage of my book, we heard of the sad passing of HM Queen Elizabeth II. I know from the various Military sites that I am on, of the sadness and great loss felt by Her Majesty's Veterans. We were honoured to have served Her Majesty, whom we referred to as The Boss.

We were reminded of the Pledge of Allegiance we made on joining Her Majesty's Armed Forces. A Pledge many veterans consider to be for a lifetime.

Our Pledge of Allegiance

I swear by almighty God that I will be faithful and bear true allegiance to Her Majesty Queen Elizabeth II, her heirs and successors and that I will as in duty bound honestly and faithfully defend her Majesty, her heirs and successors in person, crown and dignity against all enemies and will observe and obey all orders of her Majesty, her heirs and successors and of the generals and officers set over me.

Foreword

I have included the actual creation of the island itself and its surrounding reef, many centuries ago. Also, ancient archaeological finds and the political history and background to the development of Oman into the progressive country it has now become. This is to help the reader understand the content and context of these true stories I write about in this book. It will cover a diverse range of subjects in relation to my tour of duty on the desert island of Masirah, which was part of the territory of what was then Muscat and Oman. Each will have its own historic background. This will include the United Kingdom's (UK's) involvement, where applicable, which was at times covert support, in addition to practical help. Sometimes it was also not to the liking of the United Nations (UN).

Table of Contents

1. INTRODUCTION

I joined the Royal Air Force (RAF) in March 1966 when I was just over seventeen and a half years of age and served for 22 years until 7 July 1988. My 22 years did not start until my 18th birthday. I was the third generation to have served in the military. The others being:

My father Cecil George Logan[1], who volunteered during World War II, enlisted into the RAF. After his training near Manchester as an aircraft engine mechanic, he then served in the Middle East, as I did many years later. He returned to the UK at the end of the war to await discharge, which he told me was a very slow process.

[1] Cecil George Logan

My mother, Muriel Shawcross[2], from Manchester, also volunteered during World War II and joined the Women's Land Army. She was posted to the Pershore area on Captain Bomford's farm. My father met my mother while doing his mechanics training in the Manchester area, and they married at the end of the war on his return from the Middle East.

[2] Muriel Logan née Shawcross

My paternal Grandfather, Cecil George Logan[3], served with the South Irish Horse during World War I in France. He was severely wounded by an enemy shell and hospitalised in France, England and Northern Ireland for some 18 months, prior to being discharged due to his wounds. As a child I can remember going swimming with him and seeing his back, which was a mass of scars that had some very deep hollows.

[3] Cecil George Logan (Snr)

I have in my possession, what is referred to as Trench Art, an item he made, and which I treasure greatly. This is a British machine gun belt[4] to which he added a German Senior Non-Commissioned Officer's (NCO) belt buckle with a clasp at the other end. Along the length of the belt, between the brass uprights that separated the ammunition rounds, he has put British and Canadian cap badges and some shoulder pips, some of which are now very rare.

[4] British Machine Gun Belt and Cap Badges

Cecil Logan Snr was honoured by having this the main display for four months in Swindon 2018 for the centenary of the World War I Armistice. The display case[5] containing the belt was unveiled by HM The Queen's Lord Lieutenant of Wiltshire, Mrs Sarah Rose Troughton and the Mayor of Swindon. Sarah is a second cousin of King Charles III. She was Lady in Waiting to Katharine, Duchess of Kent in 2022. She is now one of the six women appointed as Queen's Companion to Queen Camilla.

[5] Armistice Centenary RBL Display Case

The round discs you can also see in the display case with my grandfather's belt are WWI Memorial Plaques. They also became known as the Death Penny[6] or Dead Man's Penny for obvious reasons. They were awarded to personnel killed as a result of the war. Over 1.3 million WWI Memorial Plaques were awarded to the next of kin of those killed in action in WWI and were accompanied by a memorial scroll from the King.

6 Death Penny

Needless to say, there are many other stories to be told from my time in the RAF. But for now, we are on the desert island of Masirah, which I can honestly say I found the most intriguing to share of all my RAF postings.

2.   TOUR OF DUTY AT RAF MASIRAH - OMAN

This memoir is based on my thirteen-month tour at RAF Masirah, a desert island off the coast of Oman in the Middle East. I first heard about my posting to Masirah while stationed at RAF Chivenor in North Devon. I had been posted there in June 1966 following completion of my basic training, or square bashing as it was referred to, at RAF Hemswell in Lincolnshire and my trade training at RAF Shawbury in Shropshire, the school for Air Traffic Control.

One day in early 1968 I was summoned to see my boss, the Senior Air Traffic Control Officer (SATCO). On entering his office, he proceeded to ask me *"if I wanted to get my knees brown?"*. My immediate response was *"Where do you want polishing sir?"* In the sixties, the Air Force was a great believer in brown linoleum products, polish and floor bumpers. This entailed rubbing the polish in while on your hands and knees, hence my response regarding polishing the floor. Heavy bumpers[7] with wooden pole handles, as shown in the photo, were then pushed back and forth to polish the floor.

[7] Floor Polishing Bumper

With a smile on his face, my boss told me it was nothing to do with polishing the floor. He went on to explain that I was being posted overseas to RAF Masirah on a thirteen-month tour, and that at some point during this posting, roughly mid-way, I would have four weeks home leave.

Before going on to tell you where RAF Masirah is located, it is worth mentioning what RAF Chivenor was like. At the time I was there, the building, including our living accommodation or billets as they were referred to, consisted mainly of old tired wooden huts. This included Station Headquarters[8] and other buildings.

[8] RAF Chivenor Headquarters

The billet[9] I lived in was a wooden hut consisting of four four-man rooms. The only heating was a coke fire in the centre of each room. We were responsible for cleaning them out, decoking the gratings and keeping them lit during the winter.

9 My Billet at RAF Chivenor

For those that worked shifts, the only problem was that coke for the fires was issued on day shift working hours. This meant that for those who worked shifts, it was insufficient. This resulted in a lot off foraging for extra coke taking place. This was usually from the officers' accommodation where there seemed to be an abundance of coke, so we sort of helped them share it.

Due to RAF Chivenor having so many wooden constructed buildings, this necessitated in extra duties at night and at weekends. This was a roster for Fire Picket Patrols when those on this duty stayed in the Station Guard House in a room of bunk beds. We took it in turns to go around the camp to check all was okay, including security. We had a bunch of keys to check inside some buildings. For security reasons and self-defence, we were armed with a truncheon. Hardly being armed with a deterrent!

I have mentioned about RAF Chivenor because on arrival at my new desert island posting, I was pleasantly surprised. It turned out that my new accommodation was a great deal more superior to what I had just left behind in the UK at RAF Chivenor.

3. SO WHERE IS RAF MASIRAH?

Where is Masirah you may ask? The desert island is approximately 40 miles long and lies some 15 miles off the east coast of Oman in the Arabian Sea. It is ten miles wide and just under five miles wide at its narrowest point. The RAF airfield lay at the northern end of the island. Masirah came under the operational control of Royal Air Force's Middle East Command at the time of my arrival on the Island in 1968. Masirah is 650 miles from RAF Muharraq at Bahrain, an island in the Persian Gulf.

Other RAF bases in the area had included RAF Khormaksar in Aden and RAF Riyan on the mainland of Oman, south of Masirah.

Up until November 1967, just prior to my arrival in 1968, RAF Khormaksar, which was in Aden, was headquarters for the RAF Middle East Command. However, with the handover of Aden, Khormaksar closed, as did RAF Riyan. RAF Muhurraq then became the new headquarters for the RAF Middle East Command.

Still active on my arrival in the Middle East was RAF Muhurraq, where I flew into from RAF Lyneham in the UK. Other operational bases were RAF Sharjah, which was in the Trucial States, now part of the United Arab Emirates. It was some 304 flight miles WSW from RAF Muharraq and 407 flight miles NNE of Masirah. RAF Salalah was 676 flight miles SSW from RAF Muharraq and 378 flight miles south of Masirah.

Historically Masirah had many names over time. These were Damorga, Orgonon, Demacira, Organa, Macojra, Serapides, Maceria. Serepeon, Machira, Sira and Mazerer.

4.   A HISTORY OF THE RAF ON MASIRAH

The RAF's first ever visit to Masirah was in early 1930. It was made by 203 Sqn very shortly after they had reformed, flying the Supermarine Southampton[10] flying boats. They landed offshore on their detachment to the island. Their role was to carry out routine maritime patrol operations in the region.

[10] Supermarine Southampton Flying Boat

In 1936 a fuel store facility was established on Masirah for use by visiting aircraft flying from RAF Habanera to Aden. RAF Habanera, (originally RAF Dhibban), was about 55 miles west of Baghdad on the banks of the Euphrates near Lake Habbaniyah. It was developed from 1934 as an airfield and was operational from October 1936 until 31 May 1959.

The RAF finally withdrew after the July 1958 Revolution as the British military presence was no longer welcome. RAF Habanera had been the scene of fierce fighting in May 1941 when it was besieged by the Iraqi Military following the 1941 Iraqi coup d'état.

WWII was in its early stages and Masirah was about to start playing its part throughout the duration of the war. In 1937 three Vickers Vincents[11] landed on Masirah for an overnight stop while enroute to the airstrip at Ras Gharim, which was on the mainland south of Masirah.

[11] Vickers Vincent

On 30 October of that year, on landing at Ras Gharim, one of the three Vincents crashed on landing. Sadly, the three crew members on board were killed. They were buried on the site of the crash with the intentions of recovering their bodies later on. Unfortunately, with the outbreak of WWII they were forgotten about. It was not until the mid-1990s that the remains of the three aircrew were retrieved. Finally Wing Commander Aubrey Rickards OBE. AFC, Pilot Officer Robert Henry McClatchey and Aircraftsman Leslie George O'Leary were given their official military burial in Muscat.

On the 22 October 1942, Masirah once again became active with a detachment of 212 Sqn RAF with Catalina flying boat[12]. This time it was to carry out long range anti-submarine patrols and the provision of air-sea rescue coverage over the Indian Ocean, Persian Gulf and the Arabian Sea.

[12] Catalina Flying Boat

In April 1942, 244 Sqn RAF reformed at RAF Sharjah with the Bristol Blenheim IV and flew anti-submarine patrols from there.

In April 1943 they moved onto the Bristol Blenheim V[13], Bisley variant. Some of their aircraft and crews were detached to Ras Al Hadd on the mainland and also to RAF Masirah. Although the squadron was officially part of the Southeast Asia Command, while detached at RAF Masirah, it came under the operational control of RAF Middle East.

13 Bristol Bisley Variant Blenheim V

The anti-submarine patrols continued while operating Bisleys out of RAF Masirah. On 5 July 1943 the U-boat U533 sailed from Lorient, through the Atlantic, around the Cape of Good Hope, into the Indian Ocean and up to the mouth of the Persian Gulf.

While operating as part of the German Monsun Gruppe with a crew of 53 and commanded by Helmut Henning, it was sunk.

On 16 October 1943, while at RAF Masirah, a 244 Sqn Bisley, air frame EH404, sank the German U-boat 533 by depth charges in the Gulf of Oman. The crew claimed a direct hit on the submarine. It was piloted by Sgt Lewis William Chapman who was awarded the distinguished Flying Medal for his actions and later commissioned. Sadly, Sgt Chapman died when a Dakota on which he was a passenger crashed on its approach to RAF Salalah in bad weather.

Of the submarine's crew of U533, only one survived. This was Matrosengefreiter Günther Schmidt, who was with an officer in the conning tower. The officer succeeded in opening the hatch, even though the submarine had sunk to a depth of 200 feet. Without escape sets, the water pressure shot both men to the surface.

Schmidt kept the unconscious officer afloat for an hour before the officer died. He then swam and stayed afloat without a life jacket for 28 hours until he was rescued by HMIS Hiravati (Royal Indian Navy) near a place called Khor Fakkan.

The photo is of Matrosengefreiter Günther Schmidt[14] taken at RAF Sharjah. He was initially taken by HMIS Hiravati to RAF Sharjah while awaiting to be sent to a POW camp where he stayed until the end of the war.

[14] Matrosengefreiter Günther Schmidt

After more than 10 dives in recent years, often in poor conditions, the wreck of U533[15] was located and the photo below was taken.

The search was led by William Leeman, the Dubai shipwreck hunter, accompanied by seven recreational members of the Desert Sports Diving Club of Dubai. The photo confirms the submarine did take a direct hit, circled in red in the photo.

[15] U533

244 Sqn converted to the Wellington XIII bomber[16], or Wimpey as they were called, while at RAF Sharjah in February 1944 to May 1945 when the Squadron was disbanded.

16 Wellington XIII Bomber

The Wellington was also nicknamed 'Stickleback' due to the four vertical air to surface vessels (ASV) radar aerials along the top of their fuselage. They were later fitted with the Mark 14 (radar dome) model. They flew their nine-hour patrols over the sea and usually at night. They were armed with Mark 6 depth charges. The Wimpey night sorties flew low at 1500 feet above sea level without an automatic pilot system to help. On finding a target, and with their homing procedures, they flew down to 50 feet above sea level using radio altimeters. At which point they switched on the Leigh searchlight at a quarter mile range from the target to illuminate the surface.

Their anti-submarine patrols continued when they moved to RAF Masirah in February 1944. On 1 May 1945 the squadron was disbanded.

Post WWII, Masirah remained an important refuelling station for aircraft flying between Khormaksar and Bahrain and elsewhere within the region. This was in addition for aircraft flying to and from the Far East throughout the fifties, sixties and seventies. This included Victor tankers flying out of Masirah, to carry out in-flight refuelling as required. It was also a support airfield for the Sultan of Oman Airforce (SOAF), as you will read about later on and hopefully find of interest and fascinating.

With the closure of RAF Muharraq and Sharjah in 1971, Masirah's role became even more important; in particular the UK support of the Sultan's armed forces fight against the Communist led guerrillas from South Yemen during the Dhofar Rebellion. This will be covered in more detail later in this book.

Also, it remains important as a refuelling and emergency diversion airfield for aircraft flying between Cyprus and the airfield on the island of Gan and onward to the Far East. Gan had a similar role to Masirah and was situated on the Addu Atoll in the Maldives in the middle of the Indian Ocean.

The Maldives is now a popular holiday destination. Some of the buildings left by the RAF were used for holiday accommodation and converted into hotels.

A unique RAF operated narrow-gauge railway was used to move the landed stores including munitions to the main base. Following the construction of a concrete runway in 1963/4, stores were flown in. However, bulk stores and fuel oil continued to be delivered by ship. This photo shows one of the two Ruston 0-4-0[17] engines while in operational use. The Ruston engines are a story in itself and also covered in length later in the book.

[17] Ruston 0-4-0

For many years most of the fuel and stores were delivered by sea and landed at a jetty on floating pontoons which were kept on Masirah and bolted together when needed. The pontoons can be seen in the background of the photo. This was necessitated due to the reef that surrounded the island of Masirah. The reef prevented ships coming close inshore. This took place between November and February because of the difficulty of landing cargo during the south-west monsoon season on Masirah, March through to October. This continued right up to when the RAF left the island of Masirah in 1977.

The airfield and all its infrastructure were handed over to the Sultan of Oman and became an operational base for the Royal Air Force of Oman[18].

[18] SOAF Takeover

5.   THE START OF MY JOURNEY TO RAF MASIRAH

In July 1968 I flew out to RAF Masirah on the first leg of my journey via RAF Muharraq in Bahrain.

My journey started on a 10 Squadron VC10 from RAF Lyneham. RAF Brize Norton, which was the squadron's home base, was closed at that time due to runway resurfacing. Together with others flying out of RAF Lyneham, we were picked up by an RAF bus from Swindon Railway Station and transported to RAF Lyneham. Many years later Swindon was to become my hometown following the purchase of a family home.

The VC10[19] was a lovely quiet and comfortable aircraft to fly in with its rearward facing seats. This is a reverse layout to that of passenger seating on civilian passenger aircraft. It is believed to be safer in case of an emergency.

[19] VC10

One thing I will never forget was the foul smell on our arrival at RAF Muharraq and the wall of heat and humidity on disembarking from the aircraft. It was like walking into a sauna.

During the brief three day stop over at RAF Muharraq, new arrivals who were transiting through to other destinations, were accommodated in the large transit billet with its three tier bunk beds. If you were unlucky enough to be allocated one of the top bunks, and you were close to the rotating fan blades, caution was needed when sitting up.

After being kitted out with service issued shorts, shirts, socks, desert boots and service issue sunglasses, there was the mandatory security briefing and live weapons firing session on the range. The security briefings can best be summarised as, *"do not kick beer cans lying in the sand as they might explode"* together with some relevant movies. They included the infamous gory medical umbrella needle treatment for those that got a dose of what was referred to as the *'clap'*. Although it was certainly a frightening deterrent, it seemed a bit irrelevant for those posted to Masirah's monastic posting.

Also importantly, there was a warning not to get sun burnt, as it would be considered a self-inflicted injury and you would be put on a charge. You would also have to slowly acclimatise, increasing exposure to the sun day by day, until when off duty you could go topless.

I took advantage of any free time to look around RAF Muharraq and would soon find out that there would be a dramatic difference in the facilities at Muharraq compared to Masirah.

MUHARRAQ'S ASTRA CINEMA

RAF Muharraq had the outdoor Astra cinema[20]. Those attending would turn up with their supply of liquid refreshments. As you can probably guess, this was in the form of beer cans. Unlike Muharraq, the cinema we had at RAF Masirah was indoors and extremely hot and humid, although it did have an advantage during sandstorms and the fly season.

[20] Astra Cinema RAF Muharraq

MUHARRAQ'S SWIMMING POOL

There was also a large swimming pool[21] at RAF Muhurraq. This had a covered shaded area to shelter from the sun. This was unlike the smaller pool we had at RAF Masirah which had no shelter at all. The result of this meant permanent exposure to the hot sun for all users of the pool at Masirah.

They also had the luxury of female company at the Muharraq pool. This was something we sadly went without at Masirah, which I will cover later.

²¹ RAF Muharraq's Swimming Pool

Muharraq would turn out to be a bit of a *'bullshit'* station and not as easy going and laid back as I would soon find out Masirah to be. There would definitely be no complaints about that.

Outside Station Headquarters stood this highly polished ancient muzzle loading wheeled cannon[22], which must have taken a lot of effort to keep in such pristine condition.

²² Muzzle Loading Wheeled Cannon at RAF Muharraq

The painted kerb stones were a tell-tale sign that the Air Officer Commanding the Middle East was based there. He did however like to visit Masirah for fishing. Muharraq also had tree lined camp roads[23]. Those posted there had access to the local public transport[24] service on rough roads into Manama and its bazaars, where one could shop.

23 Tree Lined Camp Road   24 Local Public Transport

The three days at RAF Muhurraq gave me quite a false impression of the environment for the time I would actually be spending at RAF Masirah.

My new posting would transpire to be totally different from my preconceptions. It would turn out to be surprisingly enjoyable considering it was all desert with nowhere to go, other than trips around the island to see shipwrecks or the remains of the old deserted WWII Catalina base. I was soon to find out that it would be up to each individual to find an interest and there would be plenty of opportunity and occasions to do that.

It was then time to depart RAF Muharraq, and move on to start my tour of duty and the story of my time, exploits and adventures on Masirah. Not forgetting the reason that I was posted there in the first place! It would turn out to be much greater than my expectations. Hopefully the historic facts, and of course the inclusion of Masirah's turtles, will be of interest.

6. MY ARRIVAL ON RAF MASIRAH

It was time to board the Argosy[25] for the long flight to my final destination of RAF Masirah. We stopped at RAF Sharjah on the way. We also made an unscheduled stop before arriving at Masirah at what seemed to be the middle of nowhere in the desert on mainland Oman. Here a single heavily armed soldier was disembarked, whom I assumed must have been a member of the Special Air Service (SAS).

[25] Argosy

The Argosy was affectionately nicknamed 'The Flying Tit'[26] due to the navigational radar fitted on the nose. I believe this to be a very fitting nickname as shown in the photo.

[26] 'The Flying Tit'

My first impression on arriving at RAF Masirah and stepping off the Argosy was the extremely bright glare off the sand. I was met by the well-tanned Airman I was relieving who had a welcoming smile of delight on his face. He told me that my status was that of a *'moony'* until I also became tanned. The first place he took me was the Air Traffic Control Tower to meet and be welcomed by my new boss and other members of the team.

Part of my arrival briefing on Masirah included being given once again strict instructions on how much sun we could have on our bodies each day. It included how much we could increase exposure over time until we were fully acclimatised. At which point we would be able to wear just shorts when off duty. When on duty, we had to wear the standard issue shirts, shorts, socks and desert boots. Most of us modified our shirts to tail-less, so they could be worn outside shorts for comfort.

At the time of my arrival on Masirah and throughout my tour on the island, the average number of RAF personnel was around 68. This was to increase to around 350 in the 1970s. The reason for this will be explained later.

Under the treaty with Muscat and Oman, HM Forces females could not be posted to Masirah. The only ladies allowed were those coming as part of the Combined Services Entertainment (CSE) cast in shows to entertain the troops. One such lady visiting Masirah while I was there was Julie Andrews[27]. This was shortly after the release of her film *'The Sound of Music'* in 1966, which I saw in Barnstaple when at

RAF Chivenor. I will come back later in this book to write about CSE Shows and those who entertained us.

[27] Julie Andrews

7.   ACCOMMODATION ON MASIRAH

Accommodation on Masirah for the 67 RAF personnel on my arrival was typical of most RAF bases. It consisted of an Officer's and SNCO's Mess and Airman's barrack blocks and Mess Hall. Corporals and below were accommodated in four-man rooms. As mentioned previously, it was a big improvement on the wooden huts back at RAF Chivenor. Airmen from Air Traffic Control shared with the guys from the Fire Section, whom we worked closely with on a daily basis. Needless to say, this included emptying and stacking beer cans in the NAAFI.

The Barrack Blocks[28] were built in a rectangular format and as mentioned previously, consisted of two blocks of four-man rooms as shown in the photo.

[28] Barrack Blocks

There was an ablution block on the left-hand side with showers, sinks, toilets and also contained a cold drinking water dispenser. Unlike Chivenor, this was not a problem on Masirah. No cold or wet winter weather to have to go out in! The fourth side had a brick wall. In our case, we also had a simple garden, budgie and love bird cages[29] against the wall with a ladder style feature for the entrance.

[29] Our Budgie and Love Bird Cages

In our case we also had a simple garden, budgie and love bird cages against the wall with a ladder style feature for the entrance.

John Sneddon, who left Masirah in September 1964, provided these photos he took of the new accommodation and NAAFI rebuild programme which commenced while he was there. It was completed well in time for me to benefit from. On the right you can see the new NAAFI[30] building while it was under construction. The new accommodation being built is on the left.

[30] NAAFI Rebuild

During John's postings to Masirah, the airmen were accommodated in Twynham huts[31] as in the photo, which he said were very basic. John also commented on his own posting to Masirah, *"All in all, it was an easy life really and I did a lot of reading and playing darts"*.

[31] Twynham Huts

John also mentioned that his job while he was on Masirah was, *"I worked in the Transmitter Hall (HF 1509s). My main job was dependant on the state of the ionosphere, servicing and doing QSY (changing the transmit frequency), maintenance of all the VHF and UHF airfield communication and the TACAN (aircraft location system), which was installed during my time there but had no experience or training on"*.

8. WELCOME AND UNWELCOME HOUSE GUESTS

We did have house guests, who although uninvited were very welcome indeed and helpful. Our little gecko friends were accepted as part of the décor of our four-man rooms, which we willingly shared with them. They scrambled about the walls with their sucker feet and were a great help in keeping the flies and other bugs down. There was always great excitement when baby geckos[32] arrived.

[32] Baby Gecko

There were however other guests. They were unwanted ones which we truly hated and they were Bed Bugs[33]. We had to put up with an infestation of those dreaded critters.

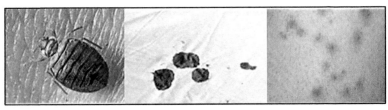

[33] A Bed Bug   Blood Stains on Bed Sheet   Marks left on Body

Despite putting the feet of our metal framed beds in tin cans containing some sort of bed bug killer, this did not always work. On waking up in the morning, there were the tell-tale red blotches on the sheets. The unwanted visitors had their fill of our blood. When rolling over in our sleep, we squashed them resulting in the blood stains. Not a very pleasant experience, and probably for most, one of the few real complaints of the tour of duty on Masirah. That is, other than mail or the lack of it.

THE FLY SEASONS

While discussing undesirables, I may as well include another seasonal group, the fly season[34], another hated time. It was another memory never to be forgotten and greatly hated by all. Once we went outdoors, flies flew at us in great numbers, bouncing off our faces, getting into our mouths and definitely just being a pain in the butt. The more we tried to swat them away, the more determined they became to get at us. We could not wait to get back indoors and escape the continual bombardment. It was relentless, particularly when they got into our mouths. The fly screens on the building windows and doors certainly came in useful.

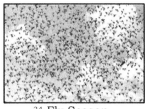

[34] Fly Season

9.   CHUFF CHARTS

One of the first things that most new arrivals created during their first few days on the island was to make themselves a Chuff Chart. Nearly everyone else already there seemed to have one so it was the thing to do! The challenge was to try and outdo previous efforts.

A Chuff Chart plotted our time on Masirah from arrival until our eventual departure at the end of our tour on the island. It had a box for every day we would be there. Each day would be crossed off as time went by. They tended to be elaborately decorated with pictures of home, girlfriends and UK scenes but mainly they were liberally decorated with cut outs from Mayfair, Penthouse and other such publications. As this was the pre-computer era, they were all made by the good old fashioned Blue Peter way - by hand. Our finished Chuff Charts were displayed on the wall of our four men rooms close to our bed space for all to see and admire, criticise or just have a good laugh.

10. THE FIRE SECTION OF RAF MASIRAH

As already mentioned, The Airmen of the RAF Regiment Fire Section and Air Taffic Control shared the same accommodation and had a very close working relationship. This included the important job of stacking tinnies in the NAAFI, so I feel I have my duty to give them, the guys of the RAF Masirah Fire Section, the recognition they deserve. The photo shows the RAF Masirah Fire Section[35] looking down from the ATC Control Tower. Our accommodation, Station Head Quarters, NAAFI, Cinema and Mess (Dining Area) is to the right and above the roof of the Fire Section. In the distance is the Visiting Aircraft Flight and Hangar.

[35] RAF Masirah Fire Section

Firemen like to keep their fire engines[36] spic and span and spend a lot of time bulling them up. Unfortunately, not so for the poor guys in the Fire Section on RAF Masirah. No matter how good their

37

intentions and effort, the poor fire engines tended to look a bit on the scruffy side, to say the least. This black and white photo shows the results of their efforts can be a bit of a disappointment to them. The photo shows this best, particularly the sand scarred windscreens. As you can see, sand got everywhere.

36 Mark 7 Tender

Below on the left is a photo of a Mark 7 Tender[37]. On the right is one of myself manning the tender's monitor. Note the clear blue skies in both photos.

37 Mark 7 Tenders

They also had the responsibility for inshore rescue of any downed aircrew, should the need arise. For this they had the use of a small rubber zodiac to perform the role.

This photo shows a DP2 fire engine[38] towing the zodiac. There was never any occasion while I was there that this service was required.

[38] DP2 Towing In-shore Rescue Zodiac

11. CHRISTMAS 1968 WITH THE FIREMEN

Christmas on Masirah was strange for most of us due to the climate and environment, particularly having so much bright sand to look at. Most of us received goodies sent from home. My Mum sent a Christmas cake, others got Christmas puddings, tins of sweets and other treats. These supplemented the excellent efforts of the Catering Section. As per British military tradition, the airmen had their Christmas dinner served to them by the Officers and SNCOs.

Christmas Day was sunny, nothing new there! It was celebrated with games and events such as donkey racing, a tug of war, football and tinnies of course. The donkeys were borrowed from The Lazy M[39], RAF Masirah's own donkey[40] compound for strays. Funnily enough they were rather lean when found and suddenly had an owner claiming them back from the compound when they were fattened up!

[39] Pat Wyre (ATC) at The Lazy M

[40] Our Donkey Guests

12. FIRE SECTION ON PARADE - CHRISTMAS 1968

This photo shows the RAF Masirah Fire Section[41] on a bright and hot Christmas Day morning on parade in full regalia ready for their inspection.

[41] RAF Masirah Fire Section on Christmas Day

This was prior to them marching off with the sole aim of winning at all costs and pain, their tug of war[42] events and enjoying themselves.

[42] Fire Section Marching to Tug of War

Does this fine body of men looking so smart and proud not set a fine example for the Royal Air Force?

Inspection over, it was time to demonstrate their marching skills to the rest of the RAF base.

In their best Christmas uniform it was time to show everyone how to march and their intention of winning the 'Tug of War'[43]. Please note that all are in step and very smart. It was of course a tactical ploy to intimidate their opposition.

They were also looking forward to start stacking tinnies very high, and of course no thought was given to sore heads the next morning. And so, the battle began with more than a little encouragement from their sergeant.

[43] Let Tug of War Begin

As these photos demonstrate, it does not exactly remind you of Christmas at home.

Also, we all blamed our sore heads next morning on being out in the sun too long!! In those days the tinnies were mainly Charlies (Carlsberg), Tennants and Tigers. The Tennants' cans had scantily clad girls on the tins just to help out the lads on their monastic tour of duty. However, it would not be very PC these days. These three firemen[44] are already thinking –

[44] *'Is the bar open yet!'*

13.   THE COMCEN GUYS AT CHRISTMAS 1968

Another group of guys I had regular contact with worked in the Communications Centre (Comcen)[45], which was beside the Control Tower. It is somewhere I visited several times daily to send or receive messages mainly related to aircraft movements. They included Flight Plans, Arrival, Departure and Delay messages, also other communications. They were transmitted and received by morse code in those days.

[45] The Guys from Comcen

Ray Flint, who worked in Comcen, provided information and the photo to help with my story. This photo is of the Comcen team on Christmas day 1968 at the Donkey Derby, which I also attended. Ray is on the left of the photo and their sergeant is second from the right.

14.   CATERING À LA MASIRAH

Having ether injected eggs served up in the mess for breakfast is a memory that will always be with me. We were told they were pullet eggs from Australia, and they were injected with ether to keep them *'fresh'*. I never did get used to the taste. However, like everyone else, you just got on with it and ate them. This is not having a go at our caterers who did an excellent job and fed us well, even down to baking our bread fresh on a daily basis.

I think most of us who were there will remember the social gathering every evening in the Airman's Mess for a toast and cocoa supper. This was laid on for us to help ourselves from one of the large tea urns. The bread baked by the mess did not have a long shelf life as the infamous *'e'* and other preservatives were not added. We were just being green and saving waste by eating it for supper. This was the time to put the world to rights and have a good old moan about not getting any mail.

15. RADIO SIX-FIVE

RAF Masirah had its own Radio Station, Radio Six-Five[46], which was run by volunteers who were based on the island. During my tour I also got involved with Radio Six-Five and was one of the volunteers that ran the station.

[46] Radio Six-Five Building

The transmitter did not work during my time there. This was overcome by the station broadcasting over a cable network to every billet including the Sergeants' and Officers' Mess. This was years before NTL and others got into cable, so maybe Radio Six-Five should be considered as a pioneer in cable broadcasting.

Everyone turned up their room speaker volume before going to bed as an alarm clock. This was in case the morning duty announcer (dare I say DJ) slept in. If this happened the whole camp was liable to be late. I was told this included the base Station Commander.

The morning programme broadcasts always started with the BBC World Service pips and news. This was followed for a short period of music and announcements.

The station then ceased broadcasting until 6 pm. Once again, the BBC World Service pips rang around the billets followed by the BBC World Service News. At weekends we broadcasted all day.

There was a roster of what programmes the volunteers hosted. Usually, the station was manned by two volunteers, a host announcer in the studio and an operator of the two Garrard record turntables. They faced each through a glass window. Each turntable was fitted with a felt mat and the operator wore a headset as did the host announcer.

The felt mat was used to hold the record in place once the turntable picked up the position at the start of the music or BBC transcript programme LPs. The felt was held with the turntable rotating and released at the appropriate time to go straight into the music or programme without any delay. My favourite was the 'late night' slot. Often only one operator would host this programme from the record turntable position for the morning and late-night slots.

Part of the procedure on Masirah was to get new arrivals to complete a form naming family members or girlfriends at home whom we could contact. This was to advise them about the request programme and letting them know how to send in requests to be played on the weekly 'Requests-from-Home' programme. During my time on Masirah, there was only one song we decided to ban. Sorry *Tom Jones*, it was your hit *'Green Green Grass of Home*[47]. I am sure anyone reading this can probably guess and understand why?

[47] Green Green Grass of Home Single by Tom Jones

There was a very extensive record library of music singles, EPs and LPs. This was in addition to BBC vinyl transcripts in LP format of programmes. This included *The Navy Lark, Sid James, The Archers, Hancock's Half Hour, Call my Bluff*[48]and many other BBC comedies, plays and light entertainment programmes. These were broadcast in series to give variety. From memory, the Navy Lark was one of the ones that was very popular.

[48] BBC Transcripts

My time spent working on Radio Six-Five and the restoration of what was to become the Masirah State Railway gave me a great deal of satisfaction and enjoyment. It was doing something for the benefit of others.

16. COMBINED SERVICES ENTERTAINMENT

The Combined Services Entertainment, or CSE as it is more commonly referred to, is the live entertainment arm of the British Military *'Services, Sound and Vision Corporation'* or SVC.

The CSE has its roots in Entertainments National Service Association (ENSA), and initially was called the Central Pool of Artists. ENSA started during the Second World War as the British Armed Forces' concert party.

They are a registered British charity and are currently the official provider of live entertainment to the British Armed Forces who are serving overseas. They have routinely, including in recent times, sent tours of volunteer entertainers to do so. This has included Afghanistan, Iraq, Bosnia, Cyprus, mainland Oman and other Gulf bases such as Masirah when I was there, and the Falkland Islands, to name but a few.

Some of the Artists began their careers in the Central Pool of Artists and then later in the CSE. These included Kenneth Williams, Spike Milligan, Stanley Baxter, Ken Platt and Peter Nichols. These early experiences later encouraged Peter Nichols to adapt them into a stage play and also a film called *'Privates on Parade'*. This in turn led to a ricochet of inspiration and the long-running BBC TV comedy series, *'It Ain't Half Hot Mum'*.

In more recent years James Fox got heavily involved with many CSE tours to entertain British troops on active service in Afghanistan, Bosnia, the

Falklands and Iraq. James received recognition for this and was invited twice to perform at the Royal Albert Hall before HM The Queen as part of the Festival of Remembrance.

During my time on Masirah, two CSE Shows visited the Island to entertain us. Now, let us try to remember the artists of some 54 years ago. A few really stand out. They were Harry Secombe[49], and Julie Andrews only a couple of years following her starring role in the movie *'The Sound of Music'*. There was also the crazy Screaming Lord Sutch[50] dressed in leopard skins, cave man style. He later founded the *'Monster Raving Looney'* Party. He is pictured below beside Harry Secombe. Others included Freddie Star, The Avons, Julie Rogers and Stanley Unwin.

[49] Harry Secombe   [50] Screaming Lord Sutch

17. RESTORATION OF THE MASIRAH STATE RAILWAY

The greatest memory I have of my stay on Masirah is the time spent on the restoration of *The Masirah State Railway* during the 1968/69 period. This gave all of us who worked on this officially approved project much pleasure and satisfaction.

At the time there were two Ruston and Hornsby built 48DL, two-foot gauge diesel engines, looking rather sad for themselves. They had sat derelict for many years. The photo is of the two engines[51] at that time – the future Kingfisher, later to be named Yimkin is the one at the front and in need of some TLC.

[51] Engine Prior to Handover

As all who were posted to RAF Masirah can confirm, there was little to keep ourselves amused when off duty. So, I suppose out of boredom, it was decided a project was needed. Doc Wagner and Tony Cox from the Medical Centre initiated the railway revival as a project. The Education Officer was appointed as Officer in Charge (I/C) and worked on the project with the rest of the team. During the 1968 to 1969 period, in addition to myself and Pat Wyre from ATC, the following were very much involved in this project, Jeff Worrall, Dis Disney and Chris Tufts.

We succeeded in getting the two engines signed over to us from the Ministry of Public Buildings and Works (MPBW) and got to work on the Masirah State Railway project. The main key task after getting a loco running was the renovating and relaying of the railway track from behind the Motor Transport (MT) hangar on the base down to the jetty and beach. Also, we needed to build seating on the flat bed freight wagons to convert them into passenger carrying carriages.

Chris Tufts from the General Engineering Flight (GEF) with some support from the Diplomatic Wireless Service (DWS) engineers, were also based on the North of the Island not far from the RAF base. They had a relay facility consisting of both HF and MF broadcasting transmitters stationed there. They relayed BBC World Service and also broadcast propaganda.

We got one of the locos going again. This was the first priority. The DWS engineers helped sort out the fuel injectors and the fitting of an electric starter flywheel. Initially we had to start the engine by hand, using large crank handles, one either side of the engine, which required the effort of two people to get the train started.

The primary objective of the project was to run a daily service after lunch. This was the time most people finished work or shift change time for many of the others. The train service would provide daily transport for those who wished to go fishing, go to the Yacht Club or just go to the jetty and the beach. It is worth noting that swimming in the sea was not allowed. However, that will be covered later on.

Luckily MPBW also gave us a set of keys to one of the fuel tin-can buildings when Masirah was first being set up as an RAF base. Fuel, including aircraft fuel, was delivered in tin cans. There was also a shortage of building materials on the island. This was overcome by filling the empty cans with sand and using them as large building blocks to construct buildings which were whitewashed.

The building we were given contained spares, sleepers, tracks, track joiners, nuts and bolts and other useful odds and sods.

Most of the track needed to get the service up and running was lying twisted in the desert sand awaiting a little bit more than some TLC. Our tools were sort of 'borrowed' from MT. Also, some tools were found with the spares. For diesel, the Station Commander arranged with OC Supply to have a certain amount of fuel lost to spillage. Strangely enough it spilt into 45-gallon drums close to the engine.

The engine itself was very heavy due to the exhaust system, which caused derailments from time to time, particularly when pushing the wagons. Because the engines were originally used to also move munitions from the jetty to the bomb dump, the exhaust system was routed through a heavy metal water tank, marked with a red star ★ [52] to prevent sparks from causing a big bang when the engine was used to transport explosives· This was removed leaving just an upright exhaust pipe to lighten the engine and help prevent derailments.

[52] Author in Driving Cab

We were allowed to carry passengers free but not allowed to make a small charge due to insurance liability issues *(nanny state even existed then)*. The intention was to build funds for further restoration work and other improvements.

The track was re-laid or repaired over the next six months. This necessitated pulling old track out of the desert with a Land Rover and sledge-hammering it straight again. We also had to rebuild or repair bridges over culverts[53] and carry out ongoing normal maintenance.

[53] Work Party off to the Jetty   Train Crossing Culvert

TURNING LOOPS

The engine was quite happy to pull but not push the flatbeds, which also occasionally resulted in derailments and having to get help from MT for the use of their crane to lift the engine back on to the tracks. This was solved by finding and reconditioning four sets of points. This allowed us to put a turning loop at either end of the track so we could move the engine to the front of the train's direction of travel. The photo shows the turning loop[54] at the jetty.

54 Train at Jetty Turning Loop

The last bit of track we laid during my time on Masirah was extending the track from behind the MT hangar, across the road to the side of the fuel can building, our so-called Engine Shed. It also involved installing the points for the turning loop there at that end of the line. The two photos[55] show the Officer I/C the project, in the red shorts *(the Education Officer)*, using a theodolite and swinging a pick axe.

55 Track extension to Engine Shed   Laying Points for Loop

I keep mentioning the fuel can buildings, so let me explain. These were empty fuel containers that were used to bring in fuel prior to it being piped into the storage tanks on shore from ships outside the reef.

The empty cans were filled with a sand and cement mix and used as building bricks to construct some of the buildings on the base. They were then whitewashed as was the case of our engine shed. This was done in the early days due to the lack of building materials.

Below the engine is crossing the road[56] for the first time to park at the Engine Shed. The restoration work was carried out after midday lunch and you could always see the crew heading towards the engine carrying their large Tea Urn full of cold water and that dubious squash we were issued with, *'Use by Dates'* how are you!!

[56] Engine Moves to New Station

This photo shows the author[57] with Kingfisher just before departing Masirah. Of note is the modified upright exhaust and high-tech bell with a pull string to ring the bell. In the background you can see the pontoons which when lowered into the sea and bolted together were used for bringing ashore supplies over the reef for unloading at the jetty.

57 Author with Engine at Jetty

By the time my tour on the island of Masirah came to an end and I returned to the UK, the daily service to and from the jetty was in full operation. Every afternoon after lunch it could be seen loaded with passengers heading to the jetty to go to the Yacht Club to go sailing and/or have a drink in the very popular bar. Some would go fishing or just stroll along the beach. We also ran a very popular night service during the seasons when turtles came ashore to lay their eggs. At hatching time demand for seats was very high.

This did not mean that maintenance work on the track and engine did not continue to keep the service running. When it was time for those involved to leave the island at the end of their tours, following their initial efforts, there was still a lot of work for others to get their teeth into.

This photo courtesy of David Black is evidence of this. David said *"he rode the train many times to and from the Yacht Club in 1972"*. The engine[58] obviously has had some modifications including a new exhaust fitted and paint job since my time on the Island.

[58] Engine in 1972

In this photo provided by ex Masirahite Niel Walling, it is worth noting that the seating has been changed to the normal passenger[59] layout across the wagons.

[59] Engine taking Passengers back to Base

This has been changed from along both sides facing inwards as it was when we initially put seats onto the flatbad wagons. Also looking at the photo and the hills in the background, the train is obviously on the return leg back to camp. Nigel commented on his happy memories of *"hacking the points in the afternoon, a few tinnies at the sailing club and getting the train back in time for dinner"*.

18.   FISHING

Fishing was another pastime many of us participated in and greatly enjoyed. We often towed empty hooks in the sea on the way out to the S.S. Electra and caught silver bream. We then fished off the decks of the Electra, which was stuck on the reef. The cargo had been iron ore so the ship was firmly welded to the reef. The silver bream we caught on the way out was cut up as bait.

We usually used an old flat bottomed assault boat or zodiac. This we kept on standby in the water with someone armed with a gaff to grab our catch, due to the weight of the fish. I had 100 lb breaking strain line which sometimes broke when trying to reel in a fish. Anything decent caught was passed on to the mess. We got a good view of the Masirah island[60] from the Electra.

[60] Masirah Island from SS Electra

The SS Electra was built in 1924 by Clarke & Co. Ltd., Belfast. It went into service with the British registered Court Line of London and was named the SS Barrington Court. They sold it in 1930 to the British registered company United British SS Company Ltd., of London, who renamed it the SS Barperiod. In 1936 they resold the ship back to the Court Line who renamed it back to its original name, the SS Barrington Court. The ship remained in their service until 1946. Once again it was sold and re-entered service with the United British SS Co., London from 1946 to 1948. The ship was then sold to La Tunisienne Steamship Co., Ltd's., owner F. C. Strick and Co., Swansea, with yet another new name, the SS Leon De Nervo. It was re-registered in 1951 for the final time in Panama City as the SS Electra by Clark and Co., Ltd., Belfast, the ship's last owner prior to the grounding off Masirah.

The SS Electra was on her voyage from Goa to Lübeck with a cargo of iron when she grounded on the reef off the northern tip of Masirah Island on 13 August 1960. This was close to the RAF airfield. The RAF made contact with the ship's crew who refused any assistance. An SOS transmitted by the Electra was picked up by the tanker Ras al-Ardh which arrived and rescued the crew who were put ashore at Suez.

A salvage attempt managed to refloat the Electra. However, it unfortunately regrounded again and broke forward of the bridge. The photo of the grounded SS Electra[61] was taken by Kevin Patience when he was on Masirah in 1968 with 39 Sqn.

[61] SS Electra

Kevin revisited the wreck site and there was nothing left apart from scrap metal. In 1990 the ship's anchor was recovered and was displayed outside the Island's Sailing Club.

The locals on Masirah fished using some very ancient dugouts that had been patched up many times over the years and looked anything but safe. This was a legacy of the punishment they lived under due to the Baron Innerdale Incident. Some of their boats were well over one hundred years old. We sometimes helped[62] them beach their fishing boats. Their main diet came from the sea.

[62] Lending a Helping Hand

19.   HISTORY OF THE BARON INNERDALE INCIDENT

The cargo vessel SS Baron Innerdale[63] was built by A. Rodger and Company, Port Glasgow Yard. It was launched on Thursday 2 April 1896 for the company, H. Hogarth and Sons of Ardrossan.

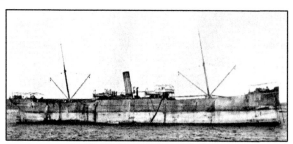

63 SS Baron Innerdale

After a grounding incident in 1904 at Al Hallaniyah, the largest island in the Kuria Muria island group north of Salalah, some of the crew of the Baron Innerdale took to a lifeboat and landed on the northern end of Masirah. There was a small fishing population on the island and the story goes that they were obviously curious as they had never seen white men before. When one of the crew panicked and fired his pistol to frighten the local islanders, they reacted by slaughtering all the crew from the lifeboat.

This resulted in a one hundred year punishment for the Masirah Island inhabitants that lasted for many years including the period I was there and for years afterwards. The full historic event is as follows:

Extract from The Times, 4 November 1904 by Terry Bate.

This may be the origin of the misspelling on the monument and also note he reported the ship had been salvaged.

"We have received the following from Lloyds:-

His Majesty's Ship "Merlin", accompanied by the Sultan of Muscat in his own ship, called at Masirah Island on September the 12th, and proceeded to make enquiries at various places along the coast as to the fate of the boat's crew from the steamer "Baron Inverdale", wrecked near the Kuria Muria Islands in August last, but was unable to obtain any information.

A telegram has since been received from the Naval Commander in Chief, East Indies, reports that the Sultan of Muscat re-visited the Island, found on further search that 17 persons had been massacred.

He arrested nine of the murderers and was taking them to secure the remainder. Messrs. Hogarth and Sons of Glasgow, have received confirmation from the India Office, of the news that the captain and crew of twenty-one of the "Baron Inverdale" of Ardrossan were massacred by Arabians on Masirah Island from the Arabian coast.

The "Baron Inverdale" was on a voyage from Karachi to Liverpool with a cargo of wheat when she was driven ashore on Kuria Muria Island. The captain and twenty-one of the crew took to the boats and were driven ashore. At all events they were massacred.

The India Office have been informed through the Consul at Muscat and have informed Messrs. Hogarth and Sons that several of the offenders have been secured and will be punished! The regular crew were Greeks. The "Baron Inverdale" has been successfully salved."

****

There is a much later account of the Masirah massacre incident regarding the crew of the ill-fated SS Baron Innerdale which was published by David Lowe on the "Wreck Site" website on 5 September 2010 which can be read in full below.

****

"On 29th July 1904 the Baron Innerdale set off from Karachi, bound for Liverpool with a cargo of grain and timber. On 2nd August, during the Southwest monsoon, in thick, squally weather she ran aground on a small, deserted island of the Kuria Muria group, about 25 miles off Oman's S.E. coast. At this time wireless was not used on ships and all that could be done was to wait until a passing vessel hopefully came to the rescue.

Later reconstructions of the mishap reveals that a few days after the ship went aground the captain and 21 of the crew took to one of the ships lifeboats, leaving 10 or 12 men on board the stranded ship, which was in no danger of sinking. It remains a mystery why the captain chose to leave the vessel or why he took so many men with him, but it is assumed that he intended to sail North along the Omani coast, using the assisting current to reach Muscat or the shipping lanes where he could find assistance. Some days after the departure of the captain, the steamer SS Prome sighted the Baron Innerdale, took off some crewmembers and duly reported the matter to Aden. The steamer SS Dalhousie then sailed from Aden to search for the missing crewmembers. One of the places she enquired at was the Omani island of Masirah, here they learned of the massacre of the captain and all but one of the crewmembers.

The only survivor was a cabin boy who was taken aboard the Dalhousie. Whether the captain had deliberately decided to land or had simply been driven ashore by the monsoon will never be known, but it appears that on landing, the crew were met by the local sheikh. The Arabs were friendly at first, but at some stage in the proceedings one of the crew fired a pistol. Whether the crew feared for their safety in some way or there was simply an accident cannot be ascertained, but in the resultant fight twenty-one of the seamen were killed. The Arabs buried the bodies in the sand near Ra's Qudifah, close to the Northern most point of the island. The ringleaders were later captured and punished; some received the death penalty and were also buried on the Northern tip of the island.

Innerdale, meanwhile, was re-floated and under her own steam set out for Bombay where she arrived on 25th December and went into dry dock for repairs. In 1943 a group of airmen stationed on what by then was RAF Masirah, built a monument on behalf of the captain's widow. This still stands at a spot that is believed to be close to the burial site of the crew, and although it is in the shape of a cross, by 2007 it had received very little damage. Unfortunately, the mason who cut the lettering misspelled the ships name as Baron Inverdale. This has never been corrected. N.B. The Baron Innerdale sank after a collision with the SS African Monarch in the Red Sea on 27th October 1914."

The British Government did send His Majesty's Ship HMS Merlin, a Cadmus Class Sloop commanded by Commander Frederick K. C. Gibbon in good old British Gun Boat diplomacy to Oman to meet with Sultan Faisal Bin Turki Al Said (1888 to 1913). This photo of HMS Merlin[64] and details were kindly provided by Kevin Patience

[64] HMS Merlin

This resulted in both the Sultan on board his ship and HMS Merlin sailing to the Island of Masirah to investigate the issue surrounding the massacre allegations.

A meeting took place between Sultan Faisal Bin Turki Al Said of Oman[65] the commander of HMS Merlin and representatives from the Island of Masirah. Because the allegations were denied by the islanders, the Sultan took it on himself to return to Masirah to undertake further investigations himself. Following his further enquiries, he established that the alleged massacres did in fact take place on the island. As a punishment for all the islanders, the Sultan issued a Royal Order. This denied all the people who lived on Masirah to have any permanent dwellings or buildings. They were also denied any other support including medical aid for 100 years. This was in addition to all those involved in the massacre being either executed by beheading or imprisoned in Muscat for the incident.

[65] Sultan Faisal Bin Turki Al Said of Oman

The outcome of this Royal Order resulted in the village of Hilf[66], situated on the other side of the hills close to the RAF base. It was built using 45 gallon oil drums, cardboard and pretty much anything they could get their hands on, courtesy of the good old RAF. Not exactly ideal dwellings for Masirah's hot climate.

[66] Village of Hilf

Our Medical Officer was not allowed to treat any of the local inhabitants during my time there. He was, however, allowed to treat their Shoats (half goat/half sheep) if required. There was an incident while I was there when a young boy got hot tar in his eyes. The RAF offered to fly the boy to a military hospital. Alas, we were not allowed to do so.

There is a monument[67] on a Masirah beach not far from the RAF Base and believed to be close to the burial place of the crew. It is dedicated to the slaughtered crew members from the SS Baron Innerdale. The stone mason that created the monument incorrectly carved the ship's name as 'Inverdale' and this has never been corrected in all the years it has been standing there.

[67] SS Baron Innerdale Monument

People might find it amazing that the monument has survived such a long time and has not been broken or mutilated in any way. This is despite the stone mason also including a cross in the design of the monument and is truly a reflection of the Omani tolerance of other religions.

This photo[68] of the monument was taken in 1968. Pat Wyre is standing on the right hand side. Unfortunately I cannot remember the name of the chap on the left.

68 Two ATC Airmen at Monument

Both worked (some may dispute that description) with me in ATC. The photo is one I developed and printed while on Masirah. The staining is caused by salt which was added to our drinking water occasionally when our Medical Officer decided we were not taking our salt tablets.

The harsh punishment order was not due to expire until 2004. However, there was an amnesty in 1970 when Qaboos Bin Said deposed his father as Sultan that year. Thankfully those days are all gone now. However poverty remained for some years afterwards following the amnesty. A very harsh punishment indeed.

I received this photo from William Cran taken at the monument on his return visit to Masirah in 2014[69]. As you can see the monument had still not been vandalised or desecrated in the many years it has been there. Also the ship's name had never been corrected.

69 2014 Masirah Veterans' Re-visit to the Island

There are future trips planned for RAF Masirah veterans to return to the islands and I would dearly love to do so.

The local inhabitants now have more suitable permanent dwellings. There is also a new Hotel complex built[70] on Masirah. How things have changed! The photo shows the hotel has a very large swimming pool. This makes me wonder what the rules are now regarding swimming in the sea. You will read later on of a ban on doing so when I was there, and the dangerous reasons for this.

⁷⁰ Hotel Complex now on Masirah

20. THE BEACHES

The beaches[71] on Masirah were absolutely fantastic. It was just a pity we were not permitted to swim in the sea. It was for no other reason than some of the local aquatic wildlife was not exactly human friendly. This took the form of stingray, hammerhead sharks and other species, barracuda, moray eel and especially the stone fish, which if stood on, could be lethal without immediate medical care. It was a long way back to camp and mobile phones did not exist in those days. This was the main reason we had a salt water swimming pool available for our use.

[71] Masirah Beach

This did not mean that we kept to the rules. Using lookouts, we did sometimes swim[72] off and around the jetty.

72 Lookouts from Jetty and Airmen go Sea Swimming

Work parties helped to unload the pontoons which were used to transport supplies from ships anchored outside the reef. Due to sea conditions, this could only be done twice a year. Sometimes accidents occurred and packs of beer *'sort of fell'* into the sea during unloading. Being early green pioneers, we did not want to pollute the aquatic's environment around Masirah. So, we risked our lives clearing the tinnies off the sea bed and thus preventing pollution. Also, being pioneer greenies, to prevent waste, the cans were *'drained'* by the brave volunteers.

It appears that the sea swimming rule was also disregarded in 1964 as shown in the photo[73]. It was kindly provided by John Sneddon who was there at the time. It shows a demonstration of Masirah style high diving off a ladder. It also shows that the temptation to swim off the jetty was just too much for many of us.

73 1964 High Diving Masirah Style

There are also some of us who would admit to participation in sailboat regattas with DIY cuttlefish boats. There was a lot of cuttlefish to be found on Masirah beaches. So, to pass the time and have a bit of childish fun, we shaped a hull out of cuttlefish. Using feathers for sails and a thin flat stone as a keel, we qualified for the regatta.

Some of us even built sandcastles to see whose would last the longest against the waves. You could call it a sort of Ground Defence Training (GDT) session or just good old fashioned revisiting your childhood.

Often we would waken up after a snooze while relaxing on the beach to find ourselves surrounded by hundreds of these crabs[74], all facing and looking at us. As soon as we moved, they scattered in all directions. They could really move fast when they wanted to.

[74] Nosey Crab

21.   MASIRAH'S FAMOUS TURTLES

As I am on the subject of beaches, I may as well continue with the story of Masirah's famous turtles which was a big and important attraction to all of us stationed there. As I have already mentioned, the Masirah State Railway ran a special night service during their nesting periods which was very popular and in great demand.

There are four species of marine turtles that nest on Masirah's beaches to lay their eggs. They are the Loggerhead, Green, Hawksbill and Olive Ridley Turtles. Each species has its own nesting season, so that on every day of the year one or more turtle species will come ashore to nest.

The Loggerhead and Green Turtle were the species we encountered most often as they nested in the north of the Island close to the RAF Base and the Loggerhead was by far the most numerous.

So, what do we know about each off these four species of marine turtles, about their habits and importantly the risks they face today? Sadly most of the risks these wonderful creatures face have been created by mankind through pollution and increased seafood demand and the resultant commercial factory fishing. Since I was on Masirah these risks caused by pollution as already mentioned and global warming have unfortunately greatly increased.

Loggerhead Turtles – The Loggerhead population on Masirah is arguably the largest and possibly the most important nesting population worldwide, with tens of thousands of turtles estimated to be nesting annually. The Loggerhead Turtles nest from May to September and their eggs hatch from July to November. This photo is of a Loggerhead[75] crawling its way up the beach to dig its nest. Having watched them doing this, it definitely involves a lot of effort on their behalf. If interfered with while making their way up the beach, they turn back to the sea and try again later. We were always very careful not to do this. While swimming ashore at night in the moonlight, you can see a phosphorescence glow off their backs.

[75] Loggerhead Turtle Crawls up the Beach

Once they start digging you can go very close to them to watch them lay their eggs. The photos show a Loggerhead Turtle starting to dig a hole[76] with her flippers and starting to lay her eggs.

[76] Loggerhead Turtle Digs a Hole to Lay Eggs

Loggerhead Turtles are named for their broad muscular heads. They are slow growing and can reach a length of 3 feet (0.9 m) and a weight of 250 pounds (113 kg). They are a long-lived animal and do not reach sexual maturity until they are 35 years old. They can be found throughout the temperate and tropical regions of the Atlantic, Pacific and Indian Oceans. They are also the most abundant species of marine turtle found globally. Loggerhead Turtles spend the majority of their lives in the ocean. Only the females come ashore to nest. After mating at sea, females come to shore a few times during the nesting season, to dig a burrow in the sand. They lay on average 100 to 120 eggs[77] each nesting. After several weeks, their hatchlings dig themselves out of the nest to enter the water.

77 Loggerhead Turtle Lays Eggs

Juvenile Loggerhead Turtles can spend as long as 7 to 12 years foraging in the open ocean. During this period, they stay close to floating seaweeds, other objects that feed on crustaceans and other invertebrates that are also attracted to the seaweed. They ride currents that circle entire ocean basins. It is highly likely they can cross the ocean several times during this period of their lives, travelling to and from preferred feeding or nesting sites. Loggerhead Turtles have blunt jaws that allow them to feed on hard-shelled prey, such as molluscs, whelks and conch. They always return to the same beach where they hatched from, even if it involves them travelling thousands of miles from their preferred feeding areas. The two largest remaining nesting areas globally for Loggerhead Turtles are the coast of Oman and the southeast coast of the United States.

Unfortunately like all sea turtle species, Loggerhead Turtles face many threats that impact their population numbers. These include coastal developments which have reduced the areas available for successful nesting. Dogs and other animals can destroy their nests, and people gather their eggs for food. Some of their primary nesting sites are now in countries that have introduced strict legal protection laws protecting turtle nests. However, despite this, threats to their nesting beaches still persist. Unfortunately, these laws rarely extend to the beaches themselves and hunting of adult Loggerhead Turtles for food still occurs in some places. Adult Loggerhead Turtles preferred habitats now overlap with rich fishing grounds, and thousands are accidentally captured in fishing operations. These combined threats have unfortunately driven Loggerhead Turtle adult populations to dangerously low levels.

Naturally, only one or two per thousand Loggerhead Turtles egg hatchlings make it to adulthood. Losses start from the time of laying and burying their eggs. This ranges from human and animal harvesting for food, those eggs that don't hatch. Some hatchlings fail to dig themselves out of the sand. Of those that do, many fail to reach the sea when running the gauntlet of swooping birds and crabs. Sadly, many natural risks of the oceans include present day factory fishing. The result of present-day pressures on nesting beaches, juveniles and young adult turtles, makes the chances of survival even worse.

Green Turtles – Green Turtles[78] nest from July to October and their laid eggs hatch from September to December. They generally nest at intervals of about two years, with wide year-to-year fluctuations in the number of nesting females. Also, they nest between three to five times per season and lay an average of 115 eggs in each nest. Their eggs incubate for about 60 days. **They are** named for the green colour of the fat under their shell. They are distinguishable from other sea turtles by the single pair of scales in front of their eyes, rather than two pairs as found on other sea turtle species. Their heads are small and blunt. They also have serrated jaws. Their bodies are nearly oval and are flatter than other species. Also, all their flippers have one visible claw. Hatchlings are dark-brown or nearly black with a white underside.

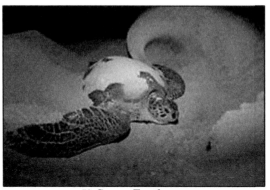
[78] Green Turtle

Adults are 3 to 4 feet in length (83–114 cm). The largest green turtle ever found was 5 feet (152 cm) in length and 871 pounds (395 kg). Generally, adults weigh between 240 and 420 pounds (110–190 kg).

Their diet changes significantly during their life. When less than 8 to 10 inches in length they eat worms, young crustaceans, aquatic insects, grasses and algae. Once Green Turtles reach 8 to 10 inches in length, they mostly eat sea grass and algae. They are the only sea turtle that are strictly herbivorous as an adult. Their finely serrated jaws aid them in tearing vegetation.

They mainly stay near the coastline, around islands, live-in bays and protected shores, especially in areas with seagrass beds. Rarely are they observed in the open ocean.

The greatest threat is from the commercial harvest for eggs and food. Other green turtle parts are used for leather and small turtles are sometimes stuffed for curios. Being caught in commercial shrimp trawling is an increasing source of mortality.

Their population is estimated to be between 85,000 and 90,000 nesting females.

Hawksbill Turtles – Hawksbill[79] and Olive Ridley Turtles nest on Masirah's south beaches, the opposite end of the island from the RAF Base and as a result we did not encounter many of those species. They nest from February to June and hatch April to August.

[79] Hawksbill Turtle

Hawksbill Turtles get their name from the shape of their curved pointed beaks, which resembles that of a bird of prey – hence Hawk. They use this beak to feed on sponges and other invertebrates growing on coral reefs. Hawksbill Turtles spend part of their lives in the open oceans. However, they are more reef-associated than other species of sea turtles.

They are up to 45 inches (114 cm) long and weigh 110–150 pounds (50–68 kg). Female Hawksbill Turtles also return to the same nesting grounds where they were born to lay their eggs.

Olive Ridley Turtle – Olive Ridley Turtles nest from February to May and hatch between April to

July. They normally nest every two years and on average nest 3 to 5 times per season. Biologically they reach sexual maturity at approximately 15 years of age, an early age compared to other sea turtles.

Olive Ridley Turtles[80] have a varied diet, eating algae, lobsters, crabs, tunicates, jellyfish, shrimp, fish and fish eggs.

[80] Olive Ridley Turtle

Olive Ridley Turtles are globally distributed in the tropical and warm-temperate regions of the South Atlantic, Pacific, and Indian Oceans. Though mainly pelagic, they have been found to inhabit coastal areas, including bays and estuaries. Olive Ridley Turtles often migrate thousands of kilometres between pelagic feeding and coastal breeding grounds. In fact, fishermen have spotted adult Olive Ridley Turtles over 4,000 km from land in the Pacific. Little is known about their juvenile stage. Their name is tied to the colour of their shells which are an olive-green hue. They are currently the most abundant of all sea turtles. Their vulnerable status comes from the fact that they nest in a very small number of places, and therefore any disturbance to even one nesting beach could have huge repercussions on the entire population.

The Turtle Seasons – At night, the turtles come ashore carrying their heavy shells on their backs. They drag themselves with much effort out of the water and up the beach. They then with great difficulty dig a hole in the sand using the tips of their flippers so they can bury their eggs and then return to the sea. If approached when coming out of the sea or making their way up the beach, they would turn back and swim out to sea. However once they start digging, you can approach them to watch the digging and egg laying. They usually each lay an estimated 80 to 100 eggs from our attempts to count as they are laid.

Some of the turtles are so exhausted and disorientated after their efforts in getting up the beach, digging their holes and laying their eggs, that they would sometimes head inland by mistake. I have heard that sometimes it was also compounded by the turtles misjudging the tides and the journey back to the sea. It was just that little too far for them if the tide was out. It is also said that they rely on moonlight to orientate themselves and on cloudy nights they can get confused or it could just be their old age. There were not that many cloudy nights on Masirah.

We would often go to the beach in the evening to turn these huge creatures around and help them back towards the sea. We also had what we called 'A Dawn Patrol' to carry turtles back to the sea if necessary. If we did not, they would perish within a very short time when the sun rose. The next morning the beach would look like a ploughed field from the efforts of so many turtles.

The Island's local inhabitants would turn the turtles on their backs at night time and leave them to die in the sun. They would then take off the shells and cook and eat the flesh. This was common practice during the 1960s when I was there and although there are now official patrols on Masirah to protect the turtles, it is reported as still happening to this day.

After about 55 days, the eggs hatch and baby turtles dig themselves out of the sand. They then start the most dangerous journey of their lives, trying to avoid hungry crabs and birds and make their way towards the sea some 40 to 50 metres away, to where they can find some safety once in the ocean. However, once in the sea they would face numerous other threats before they reach adulthood.

As they run the gauntlet in their thousands towards the sea, gulls and other large birds waiting on the wing, swoop down from above and pick off these small creatures. Not only do they have to contend with the birds, but also the mass of crabs waiting for their feast. The beach is now a mass of small black turtles[81] and crabs. The air above is filled with swooping birds. You could see the tiny flipper marks in the sand suddenly disappear from where a swooping gull caught its prey.

[81] Baby Turtles Head into the Sea

Once again, the guys from the RAF base came to the rescue and during the day were seen on the beaches helping many of the tiny creatures safely reach the sea. Some carrying buckets filled with sea water to put the baby turtles[82] in prior to releasing them into the sea.

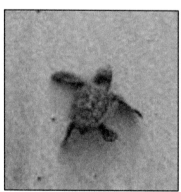
[82] Baby Turtle

Of each hatching the odds of survival are very low. We were told that some 10% do not hatch because they get too hot, 10% do not hatch because they get too cold, 10% hatch but do not reach the surface and suffocate. Of the 70 percent that hatch successfully, the majority of them do not make it safely into the sea and of those that do reach the sea, only one or two percent actually do reach adulthood.

The opening of the Masirah State Railway, particularly the night service during the turtle seasons, encouraged even more men to help the turtles and maybe increased the odds slightly of the number of turtles returning to lay eggs.

22. HILL WALKING

Walking the hills close to the camp was another activity to spend our spare time. As seen in the photo, having climbed to the top[83], I would sit and write a bluey home. A bluey was a HM Forces single page folding free airmail letter available for writing home. In those days it was the only form of communicating with home. There were no telephones on the island other than just those for base communication. Mobile and satellite phones had not been invented. The tops of hills were also secret *panic tanning* places. That is, for those who liked to live in denial of doing such a thing, prior to flying home.

[83] Author Climbs Hill

From the top you could get great views of the base, the airfield, the coast and beaches and some of the local wildlife such as the lizard[84] in this photo.

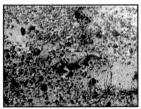

[84] Lizard

You could also look down on the local village of Hilf and clearly see how it was constructed, mainly from 45–gallon oil drums acquired from the RAF base.

This photo shows the rugged and sandy[85] features of the Island of Masirah when looking south from the hills close to the RAF base. It clearly demonstrated the description of our posting to the Middle East, that being the *'Desert Island of Masirah'*. It also helps to explain why we banned the Tom Jones's song *'The Green Green Grass of Home'* as a choice for *'Requests from Home'* to be played on Radio Six-Five.

[85] Masirah's Rugged Terrain

23. THE GAME OF DUCK

The Game of Duck is definitely a *'don't do this at home'* activity, but one that, although a bit childish and reckless, helped keep us sane. This normally took place in the evening. However, it could happen at any time. When the choices open to us were going to the cinema, which was not available every night, stacking tinnies in the NAAFI or as the saying goes, *'rotting on your pit'*, reading or dozing, updating your chuff chart or writing a bluey home, there was always the Game of Duck to liven things up.

So, as we lay on our pits, we would suddenly hear a shout of "DUCK!" from another room occupant or from someone who quickly opened the outside door of our four man room. At this point we rolled or dived under our beds as an object, usually a desert boot, a flip flop or tin, would be thrown into the large revolving ceiling fan and come flying across the room. It certainly kept us on our toes and alert. Maybe a bit crazy and dangerous but a bit of fun and helped keep the brain ticking over.

24.   FLAGS ON MASIRAH

As part of the treaty regarding the use of Masirah by the UK military, we were only allowed to fly two flags. These being the red flag at the Air Traffic Control Tower and the Station Commander's pennant on his Range Rover.

The Air Traffic red flag was hoisted when aircraft was about to taxi, land or take off. This was necessary because we were also not allowed to fence in the airfield, or even the runway. A general right of way existed right across the airfield. To protect both local inhabitants, animals and aircraft, its crew and passengers, a siren had to be sounded and the red flag hoisted whenever an aircraft was about to taxi, land, roll or take off. This advised the local population to stay clear and sit down until the red flag was lowered. Unfortunately the local donkeys, camels, goats and shoats did not understand these rules. Shoats were a half goat/half sheep hybrid animal. This necessitated the ATC Land Rover or the Fire Section's Crash 1 vehicle having to herd them clear of the runway and taxiways. Some of these creatures could be quite stubborn and occasionally bird scaring cartridges had to be used.

There is a separate tale to tell later concerning the Station Commander's missing pennant during the time of a Combined Services Entertainment Show (CSE) on Masirah.

25.   THE BASE CINEMA

The base cinema was just about the only official evening entertainment other than listening to Radio Six-Five. Although there were the unofficial movie evenings, that is another story for later on. I remember the first time I went to the cinema and discovered that the ice cream fridge contained chocolate bars and not ice cream. Despite having movies, the favourite cinema showing was Fred Quimby's Tom and Jerry.

As the credits rolled there would always be a very loud shout from all attending of *"Good Old Fred"*. This was in recognition of Fred Quimby's contribution to our sanity. Frederick Clinton Quimby was an American animation producer. He was best known for producing the Tom and Jerry cartoon series, for which he won seven Academy Awards for Best Animated Short Film.

We occasionally had an evening of all Fred's good works which went down well. Tom and Jerry was definitely our favourite. It was strange how such simple things meant so much to life on Masirah. It both bonded us and helped with morale.

26. BONDU BASHING

One of the Masirah experiences which was enjoyed by all was to go on a Bondu Bashing Trip to the other end of the island. It was considered a must and an escapism. This usually involved stopping at the old WWII Catalina Base, the World Jury, yet another shipwreck at the south of the island and is another story to tell regarding shipwrecks.

On one occasion we borrowed the ATC Land Rover[86], loaded up with rations, water, spare fuel, shovels to dig the vehicle out if the need arose and medical kit. But first we had to go and report our expedition to the guardroom, advising them of who was going, our route and estimated return time. It was then time to set off on the adventure.

[86] Bondu Bashing in Land Rover

The drive was fun and an escape from the normal daily routine. Mind you it didn't take much to create fun on an island with so little to offer in the way of adventure. It was also good experience in desert and rough terrain driving. We learnt a lot in the process such as how to change from high to low gear ratio without stopping the vehicle. In those days we also had to double de-clutch when changing gear. In addition to the main gear stick, there were another two shorter gear levers. One to change from high to low ratio and another push down lever to go into four wheel drive. It was best not to stop unless it was planned or we saw something we wanted to photograph. The ride was too bumpy to do so on the move.

We stopped as planned to see the the third shipwreck in my Masirah story, the World Jury[87], pictured, or what was left of her.

[87] World Jury on Reef

The World Jury was a steam turbine powered tanker with a single shaft and single screw, giving a speed of 17 knots. She was built in 1955, barely six years previously by the Japanese company, the Mitsubishi Dockyard and Engineering Works, Nagasaki with a gross registered tonnage of 20,235.

She went aground on the reef off the southern tip of Masirah at Ras Abu ar Rasas, on the night of

22/23 August 1961. She was sailing from Durban to Bandar Mashur in ballast to pick up a cargo bound for onward transportation to Bombay. The ship was owned at that time by the Dean Shipping Co., Inc., Monrovia, Liberia.

The crew was safely rescued with no casualties, by HMS Llandaff[88], a Salisbury Class Frigate which took the crew of the World Jury off before she broke up on the reef.

[88] HMS Llandaff

Having taken some time to take photos of the wreck, it was time to move on to our next planned stop, the old WWII Catalina Base.

All was going well, that is other than a few mandatory stops to dig the Land Rover out of the sand while en route to what little remained of the Old Catalina Base[89] At low tide it was still possible then to see the remains of a sunken Catalina just off the coast.

[89] Old Catalina Base

We stopped, got out our cameras and were just about to start taking photos including this one, when a group of extremely angry looking local Islanders came running and shouting at us. They were also firing off their ancient blunderbuss type rifles, luckily into the air. Being brave young men, we quickly jumped back into the Land Rover and departed rather rapidly in a cloud of sand. The photo shows the alleged Mosque we would later find out we were being accused of violating.

The Wadi was the only place on the island with a bit of greenery. It can be seen through the windscreen of the Land Rover in this photo with me in the back on our approach to the Wadi[90]. After a short stop, and being concerned about our recent incident, we decided it was best to head back to base.

90 Greenery as we Approach Wadi

We usually also visited the home of Sambo who was the cleaner in the Fire Section, on our way back to base when we gave him our unused rations. This always resulted in sitting outside his *'oil drum shack'* on mats for coffee and dates.

Sambo had an official role on behalf of the Sultan and with it came a lot of authority. He was the official executioner for the whole of Muscat and Oman. He often had to go by dhow to carry out these duties on the mainland. At a previous stop at his home, he showed us the tools of his trade. When he brought them out for us to see, they were wrapped in white satin cloth. He had one for each punishment, a large sword for chopping off heads, a smaller one for chopping off the offending hand for theft and another for the removal of an eye for adultery.

We asked him if he had ever made a mistake. His answer was *"Yes"*, he had chopped off the wrong hand! We asked him what happened then. His answer was that the individual was given compensation, then he chopped off the offending hand, the one he stole with.

News travelled surprisingly fast on an island with no communication systems and also prior to the era of mobile phones. This we were soon to discover for ourselves!

On getting back we were met by an arrival party and sadly, not one bearing gifts of cold beer either. It seemed we were in very serious trouble for allegedly violating the Mosque and advised that we would be *'seen to'* in the morning. I am pretty certain that was the phrase used.

Our little group of intrepid adventurers consisted of guys from ATC and the Fire Section. Being a bit worried about our future, we went to the Fire Section to seek help and advice from our good friend Sambo. We knew he would be there carrying out his cleaning duties. You will have already read that he had other more gruesome duties and had some authority on the island and mainland Oman. He was also a bit protective of those of us from the Fire Section and ATC.

After explaining our dilemma to him, he got more than a bit upset to say the least, and disappeared rather rapidly muttering away in his best Anglo-Saxon/Arabic colourful language. We didn't see him again that night.

Morning came and as we awaited our fate, to our surprise we were told to forget all about it, that a mistake had been made. No other explanation was given, so we trudged off to the Fire Section to see Sambo, who was all apologetic. He told us the bad men had been punished and were no longer on the island. We later found out they had been jailed in

Muscat. Our salvation was down to The Baron Innerdale massacre, the long punishment given to the people living on Masirah all those years ago and then still in force.

The Mosque we were accused of violating was in one of the few remaining buildings of the old Catalina Base. As islanders were not allowed to have or use any permanent buildings due to the 100 year punishment following the Baron Innerdale massacre, it could not possibly be a Mosque. It was however, being used for illegal purposes, to grow hash. This gives the feeling of being part of the whole Innerdale incident, part of history.

We did get back on another trip to see the Catalina remains at low tide. Unfortunately, I have no photos of it.

I received the following comments from Ray Flint:

"I was actually invited by the cleaner to his 'house' when they were moving. He said they moved about after a while, and flattened a new area, pouring water over it to bake it hard, then took their house down and rebuilt it in a new location. It was quite impressive, no removals company, and odd Brits who just happen to be there and helped."

I also received a comment and this photo from Charley Toohey:

"This was pretty standard even in 74/75. Every time a truck passed through the village on the way back from a Bondu Bash we gave away any leftover water and food. The villagers[91] used to throng all around us begging for any small thing we could give them. I never really understood poverty until I saw the conditions they lived in."

[91] Villagers

Thankfully those days are all gone now. Harsh punishment indeed!! This was even after the amnesty and the harsh punishment had been lifted.

27. WATER

Squash, salt tablets and drinking water; a strange subject matter you may think. However, there is a memory lurking behind this cocktail. Our drinking water was desalinated[92] sea water produced by MPBW at a facility close to the base.

[92] Desalination Plant

We accessed our drinking water from coolers in the ablution blocks in the Mess where we had our meals and work areas. This water was good to the taste. I was told that some impurities were added to the processed water, otherwise it would have been too pure and we could have problems adapting back to UK water supplies at the end of our tours. How true this is, your guess is as good as mine. In the mess, in addition to jugs of water on the tables, salt tablets were also placed on all the tables which we were meant to take on a daily basis. However, we were not all always very good at doing so and should the Medical Officer see too many of us with lack of salt problems, he had a remedy. This was to add salt to the drinking water.

We usually got notice of this by the free issue of squash to add to our, soon to be, salty water. This squash did look a bit dubious and was no doubt well passed its *'Use by Date'*. Not that we could tell, because warnings on bottles on food were not applied in the sixties. Although we did have good drinking water, we did have to shower using sea water.

Our Dhobi

While on the subject of water, one thing we did not have to do was wash our clothes. Our dhobi, as it was called, was collected from our rooms and was washed for us. However, it was done the old fashioned way of giving the clothing a good bashing and laying them across rocks to dry. They tended to fade very quickly.

The Masirah Swimming Pool

We also had a salt-water swimming pool[93] and although not as large as the one at RAF Muharraq, it was adequate for our needs. It was well used, particularly as we were not allowed to swim in the sea. It was a great way of cooling off after a hot afternoon working on the railway. One thing it did not have was a covered shaded area to get out of direct sunlight. You could also find it well used by those soon to depart home to the UK - yes the panic tanners topping up!

⁹³ Swimming Pool

28.   THE IMPORTANCE OF MAIL

Mail was very high on the list of priorities for all those posted to Masirah, as was always the case for such postings. Our only communication with home was the British Forces Air Mail or 'bluey'[94] as it was commonly known. As you can see there was not much space for writing. The photo shows the folding front. The other side was the writing space. We had no telephones, internet, e-mail, Skype, Zoom or Sat Phones in those days. Our only form of communication to the outside world, particularly family and friends, was the 'bluey'. It was to say the least 'slow mail'

[94] A Bluey

As long as we received mail on a reasonably regular basis, everyone was happy. Unfortunately during my tour we went through some bad patches of poor delivery.

At one time it was particularly bad. Someone found out that it was bagged up at RAF Muharraq and just not getting on the scheduled Argosy Flights, better known as Yimkin (meaning *Maybe* in Arabic) Airways. Despite many requests to the Argosy aircrew who flew into Masirah to check that it had been loaded, it still did not arrive. I have been told (true or false, I would not like to say) that our visiting aircraft ground crew suggested that the aircrew would have to turn the aircraft around themselves if there was no mail on the next flight in. As it turned out, there wasn't any mail delivered and the threat was carried out. By coincidence, while 'discussions' were taking place about this incident which was considered a serious breach of discipline, the Air Officer Commanding (AOC) arrived in his Andover from Muharraq to go fishing. After the Station Commander met the AOC to welcome him before he went fishing, the Station Commander persuaded the Andover crew to fly him to Muharraq with our postie where they searched for our mail. As the Andover got airborne, it left the AOC[95] wondering where his aircraft was off to.

[95] AOC's Andover

On arrival at Muharraq, our Station Commander and postie started to search for our mail. They found six bags of Masirah post hidden behind some Royal Navy mail waiting to go out to ships. They got the mail loaded onto the Andover and brought it back to Masirah - *to the delight of all there and morale was greatly improved.*

I am sure the Station Commander and AOC had a discussion about the mail issue because it magically arrived routinely after that.

I had also heard that the Comcen guys up and down the Gulf chatted away between themselves using Morse Code and certain things reached the ears of those who needed to know - a sort of Chinese whispers that appeared to work to our advantage.

29.   THE GO GETTERS

I have mentioned before, finding something of interest to do was a challenge for some guys. During my time on Masirah, a group of '*Go Getters*' decided it would be a good idea to have a Scalextric Club. Scalextric was very much the in thing during the 1960s, so they decided to '*lets go and get*'. One of them wrote to the company in the UK asking for their support and to donate some sets.

To their delight, they got a very positive response and were offered a substantial quantity of kit to set up the club. A building was found on camp which could be used to house the club and the guys asked for the Scalextric kit[96] to be sent to RAF Brize Norton for onward freighting.

96 Scalextric Kit

Unfortunately, that's where their dream ended. The RAF authorities at Brize Norton did not considerate it to be priority freight or official and therefore it never got sent to RAF Masirah. Whatever happened to all that Scalextric will never be known. A sad result for the guys and the kindness of the Scalextric Company. I think it can be put down to a good old '*Jobsworth*'!

30.   MY 21ˢᵀ BIRTHDAY ON MASIRAH

I had the pleasure of celebrating my 21st Birthday on Masirah as did many others. If my memory serves me right, it took place in the Buff Club's Turtle Bar on Monday 7 July 1969, about two months before I was due to complete my posting on Masirah. Thank you Gerry Rickard for reminding me of the bar's name through the RAF Masirah and Salalah Old Comrades Facebook website.

There are some photos of my Special Day some 55 years ago as I write this story. In the photo[97] there is one gentleman (circled) older than the rest. I remember that he was the Met Man but sadly cannot remember his name. To his left is Pat Wyre from ATC. I am on the right wearing my dark glasses beside one of the firemen.

97 21st Birthday Party

In the photo[98] are firemen including Mick King and Eddie Godwin. Although the photos are black and white, they are in fairly good condition after all these years. They were developed and printed on Masirah. They do show we all had a very good tan by then.

98 Well Tanned Guests

This photo[99] shows Pat Wyre with his chin on my head as we started to stack more tinnies. Needless to say, a lot of beer was consumed and my so-called friends succeeded in spiking my drinks. As you can guess I was not the best the next day or for the few days that followed the celebrations.

99 Tinnie Stacking

The slow pace of the camp and the understanding given by my boss did allow me to spend the Tuesday in bed.

Bruce Moyes also celebrated his 21st in the Turtle Bar.

31.   THE PHOTOGRAPHIC CLUB

Another facility available to us on Masirah was the Photographic Club. A few of us used the club's dark room to develop and print our own black and white photos. Many of mine are still in reasonable condition and used in this story. You can tell the ones processed during the time salt was added to the water as there is some blotching.

While attending as a day pupil at Mountjoy Boarding School in Dublin, one of our science teachers started an after school Photographic Club. This sounded interesting and I decided to learn more about photography. He taught us how to use a dark room to develop and print our own photographs. This small facility on Masirah helped preserve many memories of that period. At the time I attended the school Photographic Club, initially out of interest, not knowing then that the valuable skills learned at that time would be so beneficial years later.

32.   THE MISSING PENNANT

There was an occasion when the AOC's Andover came to Masirah to help morale. This time it involved the Station Commander's missing pennant from his Range Rover. This dastardly deed occurred during the visit to the island by a CSE Show. At the time it was thought that one of the CSE group was collecting souvenirs. That is, other than the Station Commander, who decided it must have been one of the Airmen. The result was that the NAAFI Bar only was closed until the pennant was returned but not that of the Sergeants' and Officers' Mess.

Unfortunately, it was not returned and we went dry for a couple of days. Fortunately, Chinese whispers did the job again and the AOC's Andover dropped in with the man himself onboard and the bar magically reopened quite quickly after his arrival.

Michael Daley, who was there at the time, recalled that it was nicked by an Air Load Master (ALM). He was the one who did the dastardly deed and was not personally affected by the bar closure as he was in the Sergeants' Mess. He was seen returning it through the Post Office letter box by the Army Sgt. Postie who was bagging up our outgoing mail at the time.

To quote Michael,

"*I took Gratton* (the Station Commander), *who was sitting in his office, his coffee on the first morning of the booze ban. He asked how the troops were. I told him,*

*'We all had a **'Stim'**! ulating evening!'.*

He didn't get the pun. Nor did he apologise when the culprit was revealed. As I remember, a lot of us marched to both the Sergeants' and Officers' Mess singing 'Balls to Paddy Gratton' and tossing Charlie cans full of sand over their patio walls. Tom and I peeled off and met the Orderly Sergeant pacing up and down the main drag. He told us he'd been ordered to stop the riot, but said he wasn't going anywhere near the Troops".

Kevin Peterson recalls that

"After the march around the cricket pitch, we ended up at the NAAFI and sat around the wall. A couple of RAF police arrived, along with their Sergeant. He grabbed a collar of someone to pull him up and ended up getting punched in the face. The upshot was the culprit got arrested".

John Brendan Brown also recalled,

"I remember it well! singing songs very loudly towards the Officers' mess patio, 'Balls to Paddy Gratton the dirty old man' over 50 years ago!! JB".

Bruce Moyes who was on Masirah at the time also remembers the episode very well.

33. UNOFFICIAL MOVIE EVENINGS

I must mention something about our 'Unofficial Movie Evenings'. Well, if you had been on Masirah at the time you will know which movies I am talking about. However, if you had not been there, then I will leave it to your imagination. They were trafficked between Salalah and Masirah by the helpful flight crews of Yimkin Airways. They in turn got to see these movies on scheduled night stops on Masirah as part of the deal. The Station Commander at the time was a bit puritanical. He did try to stop these *'cultural'* evenings and even went as far as arranging a sting to find and confiscate the material.

Unfortunately for the Station Commander there were plenty of moles and a lot of sand to bury things in. The godfather of this illicit trade resided in the Sergeants' Mess. He was very surprised when the AOC contacted him one day, to request a viewing for the next occasion the Station Commander was away from base. This special evening took place in the Yacht Club soon after.

34. WHY I WAS ACTUALLY ON MASIRAH?

So far, I have not mentioned much about what I was officially doing on Masirah, my actual job. The main reason for this is that for the most part it was the uninteresting part of my whole posting there. Most of the time while on duty, there was very little to do. The photo[100] is of me on another busy day at work! The things we found to keep ourselves amused and sane when off duty were far more memorable.

[100] Another Busy Day

However, we did have the normal legally required aeronautical processes and procedures to adhere to as part of our normal duties. This included compiling and addressing all the flight plans for flights originating from Masirah to destinations far and wide. This also required sending all the other mandatory arrival, departure, delay and other signals associated with aircraft movements. The addressing was dependant on the flight route and airspace the aircraft would fly through. All our signals were transmitted or received by the guys in Comcen which was in the building beside the Control

Tower. All signals were transmitted and received by morse code at that time.

We also had Fred[101], who was our locally employed cleaner. He was a very friendly and likeable guy but unfortunately he liked his hash a bit too much. He could often be found asleep behind the work consuls.

[101] Fred and the Author

There was only a total of 68 RAF personnel based on the island. The Control Tower[102] was one of the few places on Masirah with the luxury of air conditioning even though there were only five people who worked there. It was there for the benefit of the equipment and not us. However, we were quite happy to reap the benefits as well. As soon as we walked into the Tower, our glasses misted over.

[102] Air Traffic Control Tower

The airfield had two runways, one concrete and the other sand. The concrete main runway had normal approach lights, runway lighting and angle of approach indicators and was 7500 ft in length. It was interesting to say the least, to watch fully laden Victor Tankers get to the very end before seeing them lift off. The higher the temperature, the less an aircraft can carry. This includes freight, fuel and weapons or a mix of all three. This in turn affects the range an aircraft can fly. It all has to be calculated before an aircraft can taxi for take off.

The sand runway was mainly used when cross winds were too strong for the main runway to be used safely and also not within the pilots flying limits. It was not usable for jet powered aircraft. It was mainly restricted to aircraft with propellers.

It had no lighting other than the goose neck lighting we had to lay by hand when needed. A goose neck light is like a watering can with a wick sticking out of its spout and filled with kerosene. They were kept on a long trolley in a shed and towed out and positioned along both sides of the sand runway when needed. They were very hard to light and keep lit during sandstorms, as was the case of when an Andover flew in at night to pick up the repatriated sailor. (Later in this chapter are details of the difficulty the Andover had in landing on Masirah in a sandstorm.)

The sand runway had to be kept permanently wet to help prevent sand being blown up and around aircraft if the need arose to use it. For this, the water bowser[103] in the picture was used and spent the day being towed up and down the runway sprinkling water onto the sand.

[103] Water Bowser

Our workload varied from very little to occasionally very busy. We had four scheduled Argosy flights landing each week and some weeks that was all we saw.

These scheduled Argosy flights originated from Muharraq on Tuesdays and Thursdays. On the Tuesday it routed via Sharjah on to Masirah and Salalah then back to Masirah for a night stop. The following morning it returned back to Muharraq via Sharjah. This was repeated on the Thursday without stopping at Sharjah following the Masirah night stop. It flew direct to Muharraq.

Other than this, the traffic into Masirah consisted the following:

Support of the SOAF operations against the insurgents; British military personnel who were in the region, particularly those at RAF Salalah. There were also aircraft refuelling stops, exercises, emergencies, pre-positioning of Victor refuelling tankers, lone ranger reconnaissance flights and courtesy calls.

REFUELLING STOPS

These mainly included RAF Canberra PR9[104] photo reconnaissance aircraft on 'Lone Ranger' flights. The PR9 was the ultimate version of the RAF's photographic reconnaissance version of the Canberra.

[104] Canberra PR9

The earlier version of the Canberra, the PR7 had an impressive operational ceiling of 50,000 ft. However, as they entered service there was a requirement for a version that any potential enemy interceptor would be unable to reach. The result of the development of the new Avon RA.24 engine was capable of generating 87.6 KN (5,110 KPG/12,200 LBS) of thrust. This was 50% more than the Avon 109 fitted to the earlier PR7 version and it also had a new wing design. Their wings had an extended chord inboard of the engines which gave the wingspan an increase of 1.15 metres. The redesigned wing and new engine resulted in the PR9 being able to reach a higher operational ceiling of over 60,000 ft.

OTHER VISITING AIRCRAFT

RAF aircraft that were routing to and from the Far East and Gan included Victor Tankers that were pre-positioned on Masirah for inflight refuelling of transiting aircraft as required.

ON EXERCISE

The following visited Masirah during my time there; Buccaneers[105], Hunters, Vulcans, C130s[106], Lightnings[107] supported by Victor Tankers, Shackletons.

[105] Buccaneer

106 RAF Buccaneers and their support C130s

107 Victor Tanker Refuelling a Lightning

Victor tankers[108] were pre-positioned at Masirah and also Gan to support fighters routing to/from the Far East in addition to supporting exercise deployments to Masirah.

108 Prepositioned Victor Tankers

On this occasion the crew was getting airborne[109] to treat us to an aerobatic display in a Vulcan. From take-off it went straight into a loop levelling off just above the runway.

109 Vulcan taking off

The only one of note during my time there was a Royal Navy Wasp[110] helicopter bringing a sailor ashore from his ship to get him back to the UK. His father was seriously ill in hospital.

[110] Royal Navy Wasp Helicopter

An Andover was flown from Muharraq at night during a sandstorm to take him to Sharjah where a BOAC flight to London was being held for him.

Because of the cross wind, the Andover had to use the sand runway lit by goosenecks. It took a lot of effort to keep them alight because the blowing sand was putting the flames out and getting them re-lit was not easy. By the time we had finished, we stank of kerosene and we were covered in sand. The photo shows the Andover landing lights[111] as it came into land on the sand runway.

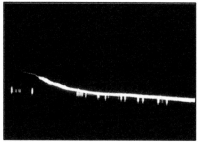

[111] Andover Landing Lights

COURTESY CALLS

While I was there a French Navy Elize anti-submarine aircraft[112] called in from a passing French aircraft carrier.

[112] French Navy Elize Anti-Submarine Aircraft

FACILITIES FOR OPERATIONAL AND EXERCISE DETACHMENTS

Masirah had an Operations and Planning Room available for the use of visiting aircrew on exercise. One of our duties was to ensure that all the aeronautical documentation, maps and information displays were up to date prior to their arrival.

A Welcome Chat – One thing we always looked forward to was the passing Kuwait Airways[113] flights up and down the Gulf in their British made Trident aircraft. They would call us up to get a couple of positioning true bearings from Masirah Airfield. They would then normally put one of their lady stewardesses, as they were called in those days, on the radio for a chat and to thank us.

[113] Kuwait Airways Trident

35. THE POLITICAL HISTORY OF OMAN

I will now try to explain the political history of Oman up to the time I was on Masirah and some years after my departure from the desert Island. This will give a better understanding of Britain's interests in that area of the world including political, financial and military interventions and support given. The starting point I have chosen is the year 751 because it is relevant in understanding the whys and wherefores of that country's development and why Britain and Oman still have close ties today.

In 751 a moderate branch of the Kharijites, the Ibadi Muslims established an Imamate in Oman. Despite many interruptions since that date, the Ibadi Imamate survived until the mid-20th century.

The Kharijites believed that any Muslim, irrespective of his descent or ethnic origin, could become the caliph (ruler/leader), if he was of good moral standing. Also, that if the leader sinned, it was a duty of all Muslims to rebel against the leader and depose him.

In addition, if any Kharijite group was declared to be unbelievers or if any individual Muslim committed a grave sin, this could result in consequences. The most militant of the Kharijite group declared the killing of these groups and individuals, that is unless they repented and re-entered the faith. Traditional Muslim historical writings and mainstream Muslims have viewed the Kharijites as religious extremists and as having left the Muslim community.

Many of the modern Muslim extremist groups, such as in Afghanistan, have been compared to the Kharijites for their radical ideology and militancy. On the other hand, some modern Arab historians have stressed the egalitarian and pro-democratic tendencies of the Kharijites.

Oman is currently the only country which has a majority Ibadi population. Ibadism is known for its moderate conservatism. One distinguishing feature of Ibadism is the choice of ruler by communal consensus and consent. The introduction of Ibadism vested power in the Imam, (Islamic leadership position), nominated by the Ulema, a learned one who is the guardian, transmitter and interpreter of religious knowledge in Islam, including Islamic doctrine and law.

The Imam's position is confirmed when the Imam has gained the allegiance of the tribal sheiks and has received the bay'ah (oath of allegiance) from the public.

Moving forward in time, Sultan Sa'id bin Sultan was the fifth ruler of the Busaid Dynasty from 1807 to 4 June 1856. When he died in 1856 there was a bitter disagreement between his sons regarding the succession of their father.

As a result of this struggle and through mediation under Britain, the empire left by their father was divided into two separate principalities in 1861. This split implies two political cultures with a long history. These were:

1. *The interior area of Zanzibar was ruled by one of the sons, Mayid bin Said Al-Busaid from 1856 to 1870. This included the African Great Lakes dependencies with an insular, tribal and highly religious tradition under the ideological tenets of Ibadism, found in Oman proper and ruled by an Imam.*

2. *The coastal area of Muscat and Oman was ruled by his brother Thuwaini bin Said Al-Busaid from 1856 to 1866. It had a more cosmopolitan and secular tradition found in the city of Muscat and adjacent coastline and ruled by the Sultan. The name Muscat and Oman was abolished in 1970 in favour of the 'Sultanate of Oman'.*

Muscat has become more cosmopolitan with the ascending political culture since the founding of the Al Busaid dynasty in 1744.

The Qais branch intermittently allied itself with the Ulama to restore Imamate legitimacy. In 1868, Azzan bin Qais Al-Busaid (r.1868–1871) emerged as a self-declared Imam. Although a significant number of Hinawi tribes recognized him as the Imam, the public neither elected him nor acclaimed him as such. He did not receive the bay'ah from the public.

Imam Azzan understood that to unify the country a strong, central authority had to be established with control over the interior tribes of Oman. His rule was also jeopardised by British intervention, who interpreted his policy of bringing the interior tribes under the central government as a move against their established order. In resorting to military means to unify Muscat and Oman, Imam Azzan alienated members of the Ghafiri tribes, who revolted in the 1870–1871 period.

The British gave financial and political support to Turki bin Said Al-Busaid, Imam Azzan's rival in exchange for controlling the area. In the Battle of Dhank, Turki bin Said defeated the forces of Imam Azzan, who was killed in battle outside Muttrah in January 1871.

Muscat and Oman became the object of Franco-British rivalry throughout the 18th century. During the 19th century, Muscat and Oman and the United Kingdom concluded several treaties of commerce which benefitted mostly the British. In 1908 Britain entered into yet another agreement based on their imperialistic plans to control the area. Their traditional association was confirmed in 1951 through a new treaty of commerce, once again being mostly beneficial to Britain. It was based on oil reserves and navigation rights by which the United Kingdom recognised the Sultanate of Muscat and Oman as a fully independent state.

During the late 19th and early 20th centuries, there were tensions between the Sultan in Muscat and the Ibadi Imam in Nizwa. This conflict was resolved temporarily by the Treaty of Seeb, which granted the Imam rule in the interior, while also recognising the sovereignty of the Sultan in Muscat and its surroundings.

In 1954, which was fourteen years prior to my arrival on Masirah, the conflict flared up again. The Treaty of Seeb was broken by the Sultan after oil was discovered in the lands of the Imam.

The Jebel Akhdar War, also known as the Oman War, the Green Mountain War or the Jebel Akhdar rebellion, broke out in 1954 and again in 1957 in Oman. It was an effort by the local Omanis in the interior and led by their elected Imam, Ghalib Alhinai, to protect the Imamate of Oman from the occupation plans of Sultan Said bin Taimur. The Sultan was backed by the British government eager to gain access to the oil wells in the interior lands of Oman. Sultan Said received direct financing to raise an armed force to occupy the Imamate of Oman from the Iraq Petroleum Company (IPC), a consortium of oil companies that was majority owned by what is known today as Royal Dutch Shell, Total, Exxon Mobil and British Petroleum (BP); the latter was majority owned by the British government.

The Imamate was eventually supported by Arab states. The war lasted until 1959, when the UK Government decided to get the British armed forces to take on direct interventions using both air and ground attacks on the Imamate, which won the war for the Sultanate.

The Sultan of Muscat signed a declaration to consult the British government on all important matters. The unequal trade treaties signed by the two sides very much still favoured British interests.

This included a group of five islands in the Arabian Sea, some 25 miles off the south-eastern coast of Oman. These five islands formed part of the province of Shalim and were in the governorate of Dhofar. The cessation of the Omani Kuria Muria islands to the British and the vast control over the Sultanate's government ministries, including defence and foreign affairs exerted by the British rendered the Sultanate a *de facto* British colony.

Zanzibar continued to pay an annual subsidy to Muscat and Oman until its independence in early 1964.

The UN General Assembly adopted the 'Question of Oman' resolution in 1965, 1966 and again in 1967 that called upon the British government to cease all repressive action against the locals, to end British control over Oman and also to reaffirm the right of the Omani people to self-determination and independence.

Imam Ghalib bin Ali led a 5-year rebellion against the Sultans. The Sultan was aided by the British forces and the Shah of Iran. In the early 1960s, the Imam then exiled to Saudi Arabia, obtained support from his hosts and other Arab governments, but this support ended in the 1980s. The case of the Imam was argued at the United Nations as well, but no significant measures were taken.

In 1964, a separatist revolt began in the Dhofar province aided by the Communist and leftist governments such as those of the former South Yemen (People's Democratic Republic of Yemen). The rebels formed the Dhofar Liberation Front, which later merged with the Marxist-dominated Popular Front for the Liberation of Occupied Arabian Gulf (PFLOAG). The PFLOAG's declared intention was to overthrow all traditional Persian Gulf regimes. In mid-1974, the Bahrain branch of the PFLOAG was established as a separate organisation and the Omani branch changed its name to the Popular Front for the Liberation of Oman (PFLO), while continuing the Dhofar Rebellion.

In 1970, Qaboos bin Said al Said ousted his father, Said bin Taimur, in the Omani coup d'état who later died while in exile in London. Al Said ruled as sultan until his death. The new Sultan confronted the insurgency in his country plagued by endemic disease, illiteracy, and poverty. One of the new Sultan's first measures was to abolish many of his father's harsh restrictions, which had caused thousands of Omanis to leave the country. He also offered amnesty to opponents of the previous regime, many of whom returned to Oman. 1970 saw the abolition of slavery.

Sultan Qaboos also established a modern governmental structure and launched a major development programme to upgrade educational and health facilities, build modern infrastructure and develop the country's natural resources.

In an effort to curb the Dhofar insurgency, Sultan Qaboos expanded and re-equipped the armed forces and granted amnesty to all surrendering rebels while vigorously prosecuting the war in Dhofar. He obtained direct military support from the UK, Imperial Iran, and Jordan.

The UK provided covert support which involved flying 22 SAS into Oman in 1970. Initially they carried out covert intelligence missions. However, within months they were leading a fierce secret war against the communist rebels who were supported by the Soviet Union, China, East Germany, Cuba and North Korea.

In support of the SAS, flying from the SOAF airbase Muscat Bait el Falage (Nest of the Eagle), British pilots flew the three Strikemaster jets of the Sultan of Omani Air Force (SOAF) that were in service at that time. They were based on the British Jet Provost, a side by side two seat trainer. They also flew the elderly Huey helicopters and a Shorts Skyvan on missions in support of 22 SAS.

36. THE BATTLE OF MIRBAT (PART OF THE DHOFAR REBELLION)

In 1972 after many months of fighting in what was often referred to as Britain's secret war, a large force of around 300 Communist lead and well trained armed and equipped insurgents, the Adoo, invaded Oman.

The Adoo's initial target objective was to attack the SAS at the British Army Training Team (BATT) House. This was situated close to the village of Jebel Ali and in the way of the Adoo's route to get to their main objective, the Omani village and fishing port of Mirbat which was close to BATT House. They would first have to get past the nine SAS who guarded the approach to the village and port.

The attack struck unexpectedly at 6 am on 19 July 1972, which will forever be a date in the annals of the SAS, akin to the famous British historic battle of Rorke's Drift many years before.

Prior to the attack on BATT House, the Adoo took out the Omani army night watch who were in position on the approaching slopes. Their mission was to look out for and warn the SAS of any Adoo movements in the area, particularly if heading towards BATT House and the fishing port. However, they failed to do so. It is thought they were asleep and therefore easy pickings for the Adoo to neutralise.

The Adoo were spotted by the SAS as they approached Batt House, who immediately took up defence positions on the roof. Captain Mike Kealy, the OIC, initially thought it might have been the Omani troops returning from their night watch but quickly realised otherwise. He immediately gave the order to open fire with their Self-Loading Rifles (SLRs) and a Browning M2HB heavy machine gun. Two SAS went to the ground sand bagged mortar position and opened fire on the attackers with mortar rounds. The SAS were taking incoming rifle fire and mortar bombing from the attacking 300 Adoo insurgents. Captain Kealy sent a signal to SAS Headquarters at Um al Quarif advising of the attack and requesting reinforcements.

There was a small group from Omani Military Intelligence, a seconded member from the British Military Intelligence and a small group of Pakistani soldiers at BATT House at that time. They joined the SAS on the rooftop and also opened fire with rifles against the attacking forces. Strangely the British Military Intelligence man was reprimanded after the event for doing so.

The defenders had one problem; their SLRs only had an 800-metre range and would not be effective until the attacking force was much closer, so other action was urgently needed. There was a 25 Pounder Artillery Piece next to the small fort behind BATT House. The nine Omani Army Special Force soldiers who manned it had not as yet taken any part in the defence battle. Because the artillery piece was not being used and urgently needed, SAS Sgt Talaiasi Labalaha ran to the weapon and found the Omani policeman who guarded the weapon seriously wounded.

It usually took between four to six men to work the weapon. The SAS Sergeant managed to do so single handedly and succeeded in firing a round per minute at the attacking Adoo, while also giving first aid to the wounded policeman. This succeeded in getting the attackers to refocus their attention away from BATT house. Unfortunately, Sgt Talaiasi Labalaba was seriously wounded by a rifle shot to the face. He reported back to BATT House that he had been badly wounded and was struggling to load and operate the weapon and needed urgent help.

SAS Trooper Sekonaia Takavesi volunteered to go to Talaiasi's aid and ran the dangerous 800 metres under heavy gun fire. As he made his brave run to get to Talaiasi, he was given covering fire by those still at BATT House. On arrival at the Fort, he attempted to give first aid to Talaiasi while still having to fire his rifle in defence at the closing Adoo.

Knowing that he urgently needed help, and of the few Omani soldiers who were inside the Fort and had not engaged the Adoo up to that point, Sekonaia strongly encouraged them to do so. After being encouraged by Sekonaia, they finally engaged the Adoo with rifle fire from the Fort roof and windows. This gave Sekonaia the vital opportunity to get Talaiasi back to BATT House and help with his serious face wound. Sadly, one of the Omani soldiers was wounded when shot in the stomach.

The Adoo attack was relentless on both the Fort and BATT House. Both wounded men had to continue to fire their rifles at the advancing Adoo. This included firing at their enemy at point blank range. The wounded Talaiasi tried to get to their 60 mm Mortar which was quite close but unfortunately died from a shot in the neck. Sekonaia was also hit twice, taking a bullet through the shoulder and another grazing the back of his head. Despite his wounds he continued to fire his rifle at the closing enemy.

Captain Kealy sent a signal from BATT House requesting both air support and the urgent evacuation of their wounded. After doing so both Mike and Trooper Tobin ran through very intense enemy fire to get the artillery piece back into action against the attacking Adoo. Meanwhile Sekonaia, although wounded from being shot in the stomach, continued to fire on the attackers while propped up against sandbags. During the fierce fighting, which included grenades being thrown by the Adoo, Trooper Tobin was mortally wounded by a bullet which struck him in the face.

SOAF Strikemaster[114] light-attack jets flown by British fighter pilots arrived around the time Tobin was shot and started strafing the Adoo. A low cloud base meant the jets had to do their strafing runs at very low level using only machine guns and light rockets. One of the Strikemasters was hit and damaged by Adoo fire forcing it to return to base prior to using up all its munitions.

114 SOAF Strikemaster

SAS reinforcements arrived and in the ensuing battle defeated the Adoo insurgents (PFLOAG) who retreated. They were then able to evacuate all the wounded SAS to get medical treatment. Trooper Tobin died in hospital from the gunshot wound to his face.

By early 1975, the guerrillas had been confined to a 50 square kilometre (19 square miles) area near the Yemeni border and shortly thereafter were defeated.

It was with great bravery the nine SAS soldiers at BATT House fought with no thought for their own safety and life despite being vastly outnumbered. Their tenacity and bravery succeeded in stopping the invading Communist led force from reaching their objective, the small fishing village and port of Mirbat. I should also mention the bravery of the Strikemaster British pilots who gave vital support.

One of the aircraft was badly damaged by enemy fire and had to make an emergency landing back at base.

It was three years before the British Government and MOD officially acknowledged the Battle of Mirbat and the bravery of the following nine SAS soldiers.

1. Captain Mike Kealy awarded the **Distinguished Service Order**
2. Staff Sergeant Talaiasi Labalaba *(Killed in Action)* awarded **Posthumous Mentioned in Dispatches.** Many thought he should have received a posthumous Victoria Cross (VC). I signed the petition raised in support of this.
3. Sergeant Bob Bennett awarded the **Military Medal**
4. Corporal Roger Cole
5. Corporal Jeff Taylor awarded the **Military Medal**
6. Lance Corporal Pete Warne
7. Trooper Sekonaia Takavesi awarded the **Distinguished Conduct Medal**
8. Trooper Thomas Tobin *(Died of wounds)*
9. Trooper Austin Hussey

The British Military Intelligence Corporal received a medal for Gallantry from the Sultan for his actions and that of others, but was threatened with disciplinary action by the British Army for being directly involved in the action at Mirbat.

The Battle of Mirbat tally of wounded and killed was:

- **Defending SAS Forces**
  2 killed and 2 wounded
- **PFLOAG (Adoo) Communist Guerrillas**
  80 plus killed and wounded unknown

37.   OMAN'S PROGRESSIVE FUTURE

As the war drew to a close, civil action programmes were given priority throughout Dhofar and helped win the allegiance of the people. The PFLO threat diminished further with the establishment of diplomatic relations in October 1983 between South Yemen and Oman. South Yemen subsequently lessened propaganda and subversive activities against Oman. In late 1987 Oman opened an embassy in Aden, South Yemen, and appointed its first resident ambassador to the country.

Throughout his reign, Sultan Qaboos balanced tribal, regional, and ethnic interests by establishing the National Administration. This Council of Ministers functioned as a Cabinet, consisted of 26 ministers, all of whom were directly appointed by Qaboos. The Majlis al Shura (Consultative Council) had the mandate of reviewing legislation pertaining to economic development and social services prior to its becoming law. The Majlis al Shura may request ministers to appear before it.

In November 1996, Sultan Qaboos presented his people with the *'Basic Statutes of the State'*, Oman's first written Constitution. It guarantees various rights within the framework of Quranic and customary law. It partially resuscitated long dormant conflict-of-interest measures by banning cabinet ministers from being officers of public shareholding firms. Perhaps most importantly, the Basic Statutes provide rules for setting Sultan Qaboos' succession.

Oman occupies a strategic location on the Strait of Hormuz at the entrance to the Persian Gulf, 35 miles (56 km) directly opposite Iran. Oman has concerns with regional stability and security, due to the tensions in the region and the proximity of Iran and Iraq, and the potential threat of political Islam. Oman maintained its diplomatic relations with Iraq throughout the Gulf War while supporting the United Nations allies by sending a contingent of troops to join coalition forces and by opening up to pre-positioning of weapons and supplies.

In September 2000, about 100,000 Omani men and women elected 83 candidates, including two women, to seats in the *Majlis A'Shura*. In December 2000, Sultan Qaboos appointed the 48-member Majlis A'Dawla, or State Council, including five women, which acts as the upper chamber in Oman's bicameral representative body.

Al Said's extensive modernisation programme has opened the country to the outside world and has preserved a long-standing political and military relationship with the United Kingdom, the United States and others. Oman's moderate, independent foreign policy has sought to maintain good relations with all Middle Eastern countries.

Qaboos died on 10 January 2020 after nearly 50 years in power. On 11 January 2020, his cousin Haitham bin Tariq al-Said was sworn in as Oman's new sultan[115].

The Standard of the Sultan of Oman

I have covered a lot of ground about Oman, British involvement, the Communist insurgency and the SAS's secret role in helping to put down the insurgency. This is because my time on Masirah fell within the Dhofar Rebellion period that involved not only mainland Oman but also those serving at Muharraq, Salalah and Masirah. For example, there were our own guys on the ground at RAF Salalah who were on the receiving end of occasional reminders from the Adoo in the hills nearby, with occasional mortar rounds being fired at the base. Support was also given to the SOAF from Masirah.

38. RAF Support to SOAF

During my time on Masirah when security in Oman got a bit hairy, particularly at RAF Salalah on the mainland regarding Adoo aggression, the RAF positioned Shackeltons at Masirah from RAF Muharraq. Although their main role was Maritime Reconnaissance, on these occasions they carried bombs. Also Hunter GA9s (ground attack aircraft) also moved to Masirah from RAF Muharraq. This was as a precaution in case we needed to support our guys based at Salalah, including pulling them out and also providing support elsewhere in the region. The Hawker Hunter, in addition to being a very aesthetic looking aircraft, had four Aden cannons in the nose of the aircraft which could do a lot of damage. They also could carry rockets and bombs on under wing pylons in addition to fuel tanks. RAF Chivenor, my posting prior to Masirah, was the Operational Conversion Unit (OCU) for Hunters.

The photos are ones I took while at Masirah of the Shackletons[116] being bombed up and Hawker Hunter FGA9s[117] from RAF Muharraq during one of those periods of tension.

[116] Shackleton   [117] Hawker Hunter FGA9s

In support of SOAF, when weather was bad at their Muscat base, particularly during sand storm seasons, they positioned their Strikemaster Mk 82s on RAF Masirah for early morning strikes against insurgents. As far as I can remember, SOAF only had three or four Mk 82 Strikemasters[118] when I was on Masirah.

[118] Strikemaster Mk 82

The Strikemaster was a development of the RAF's British Jet Provost trainer as a light strike/COIN aircraft for export. It was built by the British Aircraft Corporation/British Aerospace Company. Between 1967 and 1984 SOAF eventually operated twelve of each Mark. SOAF aircraft were flown by seconded British military and end of service RAF and Fleet Air Arm pilots. They were armed with two 7.62 mm machine guns and had two hard points on each wing with a maximum capacity of 3,000 lb (1,400 kg) for bombs, machine gun pods, air-to-ground rocket pods and/or fuel drop tanks.

They certainly proved their worth in supporting the SAS in the Adoo attack on BATT House.

Some of the aircraft that visited Masirah while I was there included:

The ***Percival P56 Piston Provost***[119] was a 1953 era aircraft. SOAF Provosts were armed with two machine guns and three inch rockets. SOAF used them for ground attack. Some were even fitted with scoops under the nose like on the German WWII Stuka. This caused it to shriek when diving to scare the insurgents.

[119] Percival P56 Piston Provost

The ***DHC-2 Beaver***[120] is a single-engined high-wing propeller-driven short take-off and landing (STOL) aircraft. It was developed and manufactured by de Havilland of Canada. It first flew on 16 August 1947 and 1657 aircraft were produced up until 1967.

[120] DHC-2 Beaver

The Beavers[121] were, as shown in the photos, painted in two colour schemes. They were used for reconnaissance, communications and supply drops.

[121] SOAF Beaver

The Beaver pilots had a novel way of keeping their beer cool. They tied a can to the HF radio aerial and lowered it through the hole in the floor to hang below the aircraft in the slipstream. A weight was needed for this purpose, so why not use a full beer can!

The **SOAF C47**[122] fleet number 301, was based at Bait Al Falaj (Nest of the Eagle) the SOAF airfield near Muscat. I remember its call sign as being Falaj One Zero. The aircraft was converted for the SOAF at Southend by Aviation Traders in the sixties.

[122] SOAF C47

It was the first aircraft I saw getting what I could only call a jump start. On one visit to Masirah they had aircraft trouble starting one of the engines. They wrapped a rope around the propeller spinner and pulled it slowly with a Land Rover to get the engine to turn over and start.

Of note, is the history that came with this aircraft. In particular the plaque on the cockpit bulkhead stated that it had been the personal aircraft of General Eisenhower in WWII.

39.   A Visit to RAF Salalah

I did manage to get away from Masirah on one other occasion to visit RAF Salalah in 1969, although it was only very briefly. I flew down to Salalah to meet the guys in the Control Tower there on a scheduled Argosy flight. The stay was cut short with just enough time for a quick hello and receive a large bunch of bananas to take back with me in exchange for some Masirah Crayfish. Salalah had come under attack from the Adoo insurgents with a few mortar shells being lobbed at the base.

It was post haste back on board the Argosy and a very quick take off back to Masirah before any damage was done to the aircraft. The bananas arrived safely back on Masirah and enjoyed.

There had been some slight damage to the Argosy's brakes from the mortar attack but with a decent length runway at Masirah and a lot of flat sun-baked sand in the runway overshoot area, there wasn't any real problem for our landing back on Masirah. In fact, the Argosy only needed the runway.

I only managed to take one photo during that brief visit which was of the Salalah deterrent[123] shown below.

[123] Salalah Deterrent

I believe It was possibly meant to scare off the insurgents, the Adoo. Once again good use was made of old 45-gallon oil drums. These were topped by a waste bin and a funnel for a nose cone. The side tubes came from fuel bowser side tubes that stored the fuel pipes. The fins were wooden with bowser tubes topped with old headlight casings. No one can accuse the RAF of being anything other than resourceful.

Geoff Wilson remembers the missile well when he was on an aerial servicing visit from Sharjah, sometime in 1968/69 when it appeared. He remembers that there may have been a little concern that it might appear to be a little provocative to the Adoo. On his second tour to Masirah in 1975, he visited Salalah again and found the same missile sticking up in a rubbish dump of military equipment.

40. MY EYE PROBLEM AND A VISIT BACK TO RAF MUHARRAQ

The brightness and glare caused me problems during my tour on Masirah and resulted in a trip back to Muharraq to visit the RAF Hospital. The service issue sunglasses previously mentioned were not up to the job and I developed dry eye syndrome. This was caused by the glare of the sun on the sand. The optometrist in Muharraq prescribed very dark tinted corrective lens glasses and untinted for night time. I had to hang around for a few days to pick them up.

This gave me the opportunity to visit downtown Manama, have a look around and pick up a few souvenirs. After my few days there it was time to go back to the desert island of Masirah.

On my arrival back there was an unpleasant surprise! My trip to RAF Muharraq was followed by the bill for the glasses in the form of a deduction from pay. Needless to say, I was not amused. Something didn't seem right!

41. MASIRAH'S HISTORICAL BACKGROUND

Masirah's early history can be traced back to the Neolithic, Bronze Age and Iron Age. Archaeological sites are located all over the island. One study found shell middens (a mound of domestic refuse, containing shells and animal bones marking the site of a prehistoric settlement), dating to 6000 BCE. Stone axes from 3000 BCE and fish line sinkers from 4000 BCE were also found.

The Magan Civilization, also known as 'Makkan', was an ancient region in what is now modern-day United Arab Emirates and Oman with archaeological records dating from 2000–2700 BCE.

Indus region pottery shards and local copper mining in small quantities can be dated to 1500 BCE.

The Island was also occupied by the Portuguese navy in the sixteenth century. What little is known about the island's modern history indicates that the island's fishermen were accomplished sailors, who constructed their own boats, and traded with the mainland.

42. THE GEOLOGY OF THE DESERT ISLAND OF MASIRAH

The rugged terrain of the island and surrounding rough coastline has led to the appearance of many wrecked dhows on the beaches of the island, most of them well preserved by the salt water and intense heat. In addition to the shipwrecks on the reef already mentioned, there was amongst others the USS Peacock which grounded on 21 September 1835.

The environment of the ocean bottom that surrounds the island is very hostile. This is due to most of the ocean floor being covered in either sand or hard rock. There is a swift current that flows through the area and there is also a very sharp halocline visible on the surf of the sea. A halocline is a vertical zone in oceanic water that is particularly well developed around Masirah. Within the zone, the salinities decrease by several parts per thousand from the base of the surface layer to the bottom of the sea.

On Masirah an Ophiolite is a section of Earth's oceanic crust where the underlying upper mantle has been lifted up. In the process of this occurring, it was exposed above sea level. It was then placed onto the continental crustal rocks.

This resulted in the ocean floor environment, which surrounds Masirah, becoming hostile due to the majority of the area being covered in either sand or hard rock. There is also a swift current flowing through the area with a very sharp halocline visible on the surface of the ocean.

In addition to the choppy surface conditions, and also because the water depth nearby is only around ten metres, it is not conducive to side-scan sonar searches.

Despite the inadequate quality of the ocean floor around Masirah, it is however, surprisingly, a remarkably successful breeding area for a wide range of marine life, particularly fish. Also, any hard discarded objects on the seabed, such as barrels, other such debris and local fauna quickly colonised.

During the summer months there is normally a constant strong wind which creates large waves on the sea. This explains why the supply ships for the RAF base had to anchor outside the surrounding reef and could only be unloaded between the months of November and February, using a pontoon of bolted together sections to cross over the reef to the jetty.

The storms created by this phenomenon can be quite severe. For example, they were so bad, that in June 2007 it resulted in the temporary evacuation of some 7,000 people from their Masirah homes due to the high storm waves produced by the powerful Cyclone Gonu. This was the strongest storm to have hit the Persian Gulf region in 60 years.

The Island of Masirah is almost entirely composed of highly faulted rock due to the arrangement of mineral grains in the sediments. The folded ophiolite complex is unconformably overlain by unfolded Eocene limestone. This is correlated with the upper cretaceous semail complex of the Oman mainland.

The ophiolites include serpentine, basalt, pyroclastic and some radiolarite, and intrusive complexes largely composed of serpentine, peridotite, picrite, anorthosite, gabbro and granite, with transitional varieties.

Emplacement structures within the intrusions are extremely complicated, with the gabbros full of blocks, mostly of serpentine up to 1 km or more in diameter. There are also late-stage veins, lenses and irregular bodies of granite. Ophiolites, probably derived from the mantle, are ultrabasic differentiates with soda metasomatism. Tectonic structures are largely pre-Eocene. They include fractures, some of which are parallel to the late Tertiary submarine Masirah fault which is related to the continental drift.

43. FAREWELL MASIRAH

Well I think I have just about exhausted my 'Masirah Memories'. I enjoyed my time and experiences whilst there. As you will have seen, there was also intrigue. I was kept busy, surprisingly more so when not on duty, and never really bored. It was now time for a few of us to board the Argosy for our final Yimkin Airways flight to Muharraq.

THE NO-NOOKIE TIE

Unlike Masirah's monastic posting, all who were stationed there were unaccompanied. In adddition there was also the Omani ban on female postings there. Muharraq was accompanied (families) other than for the single guys. However, they did not go without female company as was evident in the Muharraq swimming pool photo previously shown. This meant they did not get a *'No-Nookie Tie'*[124] at the end of their tour. The tie was presented to those who were posted to RAF Masirah and completed their full tour on the island just prior to their departure back to the UK.

This is mine which I received in 1969 and that I still have in my possession. In case you have trouble understanding the logo[125] on the tie, it is the female sex symbol. On the inside there is a red minus and the number twelve is in Latin above. This represents the twelve months monastic period spent on the desert island of Masirah without female company. Well, let's say that is the polite definition!

124 No Nookie Tie

125 The Logo

UK BOUND

On our arrival at Muharraq, there sitting on the pan awaiting us was a lovely 10 Squadron VC10[126] our carriage home. We could not wait to check in, board and get going.

126 10 Squadron VC10

163

BYE BYE BAHRAIN

It was bye bye to Bahrain[127]. I took this photo on the climb after take off. Next was a brief stop at RAF Akrotiri on Cyprus to refuel before continuing on to the UK. We landed at Manchester Airport because the majority of the other passengers were from the Cheshire Regiment.

[127] Farewell Bahrain

As we pulled into the gate, I saw an Aer Lingus BAC111 alongside. My father had sent me an open Aer Lingus ticket to Dublin. Great I thought, as I was a transit passenger, I could quickly go straight to the departure desk and catch that flight to Dublin for my official 21st Birthday Party and disembarkation leave.

Alas, it was not to be. Despite showing my ticket to Dublin, I was made queue up with the rest by the Army Disembarkation Team and made go through emigration and customs. By the time I had done all this, I saw the BAC111 taxi out and it was the last flight to Dublin that evening. So, it was a thank you *Jobs Worth!* Because I was going straight to Dublin, and not my next posting to RAF Valley in Anglesey, all my RAF uniforms and kit had been boxed up and dispatched from RAF Masirah to RAF Valley.

Luckily my Grandparents, on my mother's side, came from Longsight in Manchester and that is where I headed for that night. I had no way of pre-warning them of my imminent arrival so they had a pleasant surprise when I knocked on their door, and that was for all three of us. After an enjoyable evening with my Grandparents, it was back to Manchester's Ringway Airport and my flight home to Dublin.

I must say, however, that I remember more of my 21st birthday on Masirah than my belated one in Dublin, and I am not inclined to say, sadly either! Masirah was something special with so many memories.

After my leave it was time to board the Dun Laoghaire to Holyhead Mail Boat to take up my next posting at RAF Valley in Anglesey. This was prior to the car ferry service being established. On arrival at RAF Valley, there was a problem. The box containing my military clothing had not arrived from RAF Masirah. The Station Warrant Officer was not amused and certainly let me know. I had to go through the arrival process which involved going around RAF Valley with my arrival *chit* to get signed by everyone and their dog. This required repeated explanations of why I was not in uniform at every location. My new boss in ATC, the SATCO was a bit more understanding. Luckily it arrived a week later.

Because RAF Valley was a Flight Training base we did not work at weekends. So, I frequently took trips back to Dublin where I would meet with an old school friend, Gordon Campbell. We would, as they say in Ireland, *'go on the lash'*. In other words, go on a pub crawl often ending up at Old Wesley Rugby Club.

It was on one of my visits to the Rugby Club that I met Daphne Foster. She was helping behind the bar and was serving me. When I asked for crisps, she asked if I was getting a pack for her as well. I agreed on condition she had a dance with me. She did, and encouraged by her friend Iris Stewart to stay with me, until the end of the evening, this she did. At the end of the evening we agreed to meet up the following weekend and go to the pictures.

We met up most weekends after that and in time ended up getting married[128] in Dublin at St. Mary's Church, Crumlin on 26 February 1972.

[128] Our Wedding Day

Surprisingly it turned out that our fathers knew each other. Also, Daphne's father used to go fishing with my Great Uncle Tommy Logan at Portrane, a small seaside village north of Dublin. My uncle Jimmy, my father's brother, had converted an old railway carriage into a holiday home in a field at Portrane. In the next field which had the sand dunes, which ran down to the sandy beach, was the pump for fresh water. There was also a black Nissan Hut just before the sand dunes where, by co-incidence, Daphne and her family holidayed during the summer school holidays. Daphne and I must have passed each other umpteen times going to and from the beach, when playing on the beach or swimming. It is certainly a strange world. Was it fate that years later when we were adults, we were to meet in the Rugby Club?

After over 51 years of marriage as I write this book, Daf is still putting up with me despite the long Covid Pandemic period we went through; in particular, during that time, the stress of continuous phone calls advising us of the passing of people with Parkinson's, many being friends.

Twenty years ago I was diagnosed with Parkinson's Disease. Daf is now my carer. This brings an uncertain future for us. More especially after all she has witnessed and been told about the disease over many years. Add to this, the separation, stress and worry associated with being a HM Forces military wife that spouses have to go through. She is my rock.

It seems surreal and some coincidence that the editor of this book is the very same Iris Stewart, now Buchanan after her marriage to Cecil.

AFTERTHOUGHT

I find it still hard to believe that more than fifty five years have flown by since I first arrived on Masirah, that magical island off the coast of the then Muscat and Oman, now just Oman. I also believe that the magic was only really appreciated after the tour ended and I found myself back to the more mundane life of a regular RAF base.

This handmade gift[129] was given to me by a Local Villager on my departure from the island. It is something I still have in my possession and which I will always treasure.

It was amazing that those posted to the island found so many things to occupy themselves with and crammed so much in during their tour of duty there. I have found very few Masirah veterans who did not enjoy their time spent on that desert island and did not have pleasant memories. It may not be surprising for you to find that the translation of the motto on the RAF Masirah crest of *'AL-I TIMAD ALA-NAFS'* is Self-Reliance.

44. Postings

Following my tour at RAF Masirah and posting to RAF Valley, and prior to our wedding, I was posted again, this time to RAF Heathrow Radar which was at the side of Heathrow Airport. My accommodation was at RAF West Drayton. Prior to getting married I had to get my banns read. This involved getting the plans of my accommodation at RAF West Drayton. The reason? A parish boundary ran right through the middle of the four-man room I was in. We had to determine which parish my bed was in, so I went to the correct church to get my banns read. No doubt you will find this hardly believable!

While at RAF Heathrow Radar we got married and Daphne and I moved into a brand new Married Quarter at RAF Uxbridge. It was right beside the Band of The Royal Air Force School of Music. From RAF Heathrow Radar, the RAF moved into the newly opened London Air Traffic Control Centre Military (LATCC Mil) in West Drayton. It was while here that our son Paul was born on 18 January 1973 and then we were three.

LATCC Mil covered the whole of the south of the UK other than the airways and the control areas around airfields. It was very hi-tech for its time, with touch screen computers and radar heads, both primary and secondary, at various places around the south of England.

For those readers who are wondering what is the difference between primary and secondary radar, I will explain.

Primary radar sends a signal out, which on contact with an aircraft, bounces back, and appears as a blip on the radar screen showing the position of aircraft. Secondary radar picks up the signals generated by aircrafts' onboard equipment, the transponders. This signal is picked up by a smaller narrower rectangular radar head that is located on top of the larger primary radar head or is stand alone. The big advantage of secondary radar is it transmits information that appears beside the blip seen on the radar screen. This shows the aircraft's call sign, its height and where it has come from and going to using International Commercial Aeronautical Organisation (ICAO) codes of the airfield concerned, e.g. LGTW for London Gatwick. It can also, in an emergency, show the relevant information to alert controllers on their screens of their emergency information such as Hi-Jack, Rt-Fail, SOS.

From there I was posted to 4 Sqn Harriers at RAF Wildenrath in Germany. 4 Sqn was one of three Harrier squadrons based there that formed the RAF Germany Harrier Force during the Cold War.

Daphne and Paul joined me in Germany when we moved into Married Quarters in Geilenkirchen.

Our daughter Susan was born in the British Military Hospital at Wegberg on 11 April 1976. I remember driving her home from the hospital and being stopped in the small German village of Heinsberg and given hand painted boiled eggs for Easter.

The entire Harried Force was moved to RAF Gütersloh when their runway there was being re-surfaced. The RAF Phantoms based there, moved to RAF Wildenrath. The Harriers could manage without a hard surface normal runway.

This meant a move to yet another Married Quarters in the small town of Rheda-Wiedenbrück right across the road from the railway station.

While with 4 Sqn, we flew to the Italian Air Force Base in Decimomannu, Sardinia for an annual Armament Practice Camp (APC) to use the live NATO Bombing Range off the Sardinian coast.

While at RAF Gütersloh I was promoted to Corporal and transferred to Air Traffic Control (ATC) there. My main duties in ATC included manning the Runway Safety Caravan which was close to the touch down point of the runway. This was quite a busy and tiring job on a busy fighter station.

The work involved checking aircraft had their wheels down coming into land. This was done by listening in on the local frequency to ensure pilots called 'three greens' when calling 'finals' in the visual circuit on their approach to the runway. This was done in case the Local Controller missed the fact that the pilot had not made the 'three greens' call, because this was confirmation by the pilot that the aircraft undercarriage was down and locked.

We also listened in to ensure the Radar Talk Down Controller confirmed three greens at his three miles to go call to the Local Controller on a straight in radar approach to the runway. If not, we interrupted with a 'Confirm Greens' call and if needed, we pressed the button that fired a red Vary Flare to make the pilot pull up and go around for another approach to the runway.

At night we watched to ensure we could see the aircraft landing light was on when on finals. This came on when the nose wheel was down and locked. Unless the pilot pre-advised that he was doing a practice no light approach, or if in daytime, the pilot had called *'three greens'*, and on a visual inspection with binoculars it could be seen that the wheels were not fully down, a red flare was fired.

Prior to entering the runway, visual inspections of aircraft were made prior to take off. These included checking for loose or open panels, leaks, red flags attached to pins that should have been removed prior to taxi and generally anything unusual or suspicious. If required, the pilot was asked to return to dispersal. If time permitted, ground crew came to the aircraft to fix the problem. If no smoke was seen, the aircraft was shut down and towed away. If it was on fire, the crash crew came to the aircraft to ensure the ejector seat pins had been inserted, prior to helping the pilot out of the aircraft, if required.

The other role while in ATC that was unique to the Harrier, was Harrier Mobile in a Land Rover equipped with a transmitter and receiver on the Local Control Tower Frequency and places to plug in Very Pistols.

Part of this role was to inspect the maxi pad which was a square of metal strips that interlocked with each other. It was just big enough for a Harrier to land on. Part of the inspection each day was to inspect that the pins that had been hammered in to secure the pad to the ground were not loose. If this was the case we used a sledge hammer to knock them back into place. We also had to check that the pin lock down point had not cracked. If so, we moved the pin to a new location. We also carried out this inspection every ten vertical landings or take offs. For safety reasons we generally kept the Land Rover in reverse gear in case the aircraft drifted over towards us. If the aircraft did go over the top of the Land Rover while hovering, it could result in the vehicle and its occupants being turned upside down. If it was thought this was going to happen, we advised the pilot on the local tower frequency *'that he was missing the pad and the press up'*.

Often, when an aircraft on a test flight after maintenance was hovering over the pad, the pilot would request that we *'check the nozzle angle'*. This was done by looking at lines on the aircraft fuselage outward from the engine nozzle rotation points. Then, using binoculars, checked them against a single line on the nozzles. Usually, it was for the vertical straight down line or one either side of it. For safety purposes, we also visually checked the aircraft. On one occasion when the aircraft had landed, I saw smoke coming out of the Gas Turbine Starter (GTS) vents at the rear of the cockpit. I advised the pilot to shut down and the crash crew was called, but there was no fire. The aircraft was towed away and the same happened twice more after inspection of the aircraft by engineers back at dispersal. By the third time, the engineers thought I was seeing things. However, on deeper inspection they found that an oil pipe that ran across the top of the GTS exhaust had a hairline fracture. On landing and with the engine winding down, it caused the pipe to flex and leak oil on to the GTS exhaust pipe. The squadron finally admitted that the aircraft had a serious fault.

My other postings while in the RAF included RAF Brize Norton, HQNI in Lisburn, RAF Coltishall, RAF Marham, RAF Odiham (twice, while with 7 Sqn Chinook) and also as a Base Duty Operations Controller, Port San Carlos in the Falklands with 7 Sqn Chinook Detachment (ChinDet).

Needless to say, there are many other stories to be told from my time in the RAF. But for now, we are on the desert island of Masirah, which I can honestly say I found the most intriguing to share of all my RAF postings.

ABOUT THE AUTHOR

During my eight year tenure volunteering as Chair of Parkinson's UK Swindon and District Branch, the services and support for both those with Parkinson's and their carers was greatly improved. This resulted in both Daphne and I having the honour of being invited to HM The Queen's Garden Party as a result of the Swindon Branch being awarded The Queen's Award for Voluntary Service[130]. This is the equivalent of an MBE for Charities.

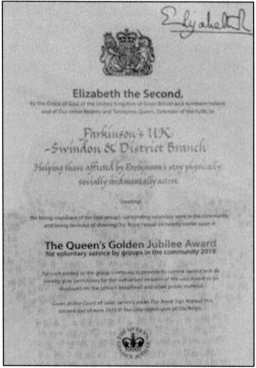

[130] Queen's Award for Voluntary Service

This was also the last Garden Party[131] Her Majesty attended. The photo was taken by Daphne.

[131] The Queen at Garden Party

In 2021 I was awarded Parkinson's UK's Volunteer of the Year Gold Parkinson's Brain Pin Badge[132].

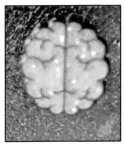

[132] Parkinson's Gold Pin

In 2022 I was nominated for and received the Mayor of Swindon's Pride Award[133] for outstanding services to the People of Swindon in a ceremony in Swindon Town's Football Club's large function room.

[133] Pride of Swindon Award

While a representative of those affected by Parkinson's in the Swindon area on the NHS's Clinical Commissioning Group's Committee, we successfully established the Swindon Parkinson's Services Team at Swindon Great Western Hospital (GWH). The team consisted of Parkinson's Specialist Nurses, Consultants, Physiotherapists, Speech & Language and Occupational Health. GWH now being one of the few hospitals with such a dedicated team.

My personal campaign took nearly four years to get a self-medication procedure introduced into GWH. This was done in support of PUK's National *'Get It On Time'* medication campaign. As a patient I have found the procedure works extremely well and is easy to use. This campaign was supported by Sir Robert Buckland MP, particularly during the trial phase.

The *Patient Self-Administration of Medication Procedure* allows those patients who are deemed capable of managing their own medication while in hospital to do so. It has existed in Swindon's GWH for at least the past five years.

So how and why was this procedure introduced? Prior to the introduction, the then Swindon Parkinson's Branch had over some years tried various ways of improving *'Get It On Time'*. This included the purchase of two Pill Timers for each ward to be used when Parkinson's patients were on that ward. This included giving *'Get It On Time'* talks at GWH. Unfortunately, this was not successful, and the timers gradually disappeared.

I was Branch Chair at this time and decided to carry out a search of UK Hospitals to see if any allowed their Parkinson's patients to manage their own medication. I found that there were NHS Hospitals that did. I was able to download some of their procedures. These I emailed to GWH asking why they did not have such procedures. When finally GWH started a trial period, I requested my MP to support me by forwarding my emails to GWH checking on progress. This Sir Robert did by passing it through his Parliamentary Private Secretary in Westminster. This aim was to put pressure on getting the procedure into GWH.

As I mentioned at the start, such a procedure does exist at GWH. If on any occasion, a patient capable of *'self-medicating'* is told such a procedure does not exist, just quote its name to the person concerned:

<u>GWH Patient Self-Administration of Medication</u>

ACKNOWLEDGEMENTS

I would like to start by thanking my dear friend Iris Buchanan, for her much valued and patiently given support in editing this book. Words alone cannot express my gratitude to Iris for her valuable advice and support in taking on the editorial role. My thanks also to Cecil Buchanan for his skill in improving the quality of some old photographs. All of which was freely given.

I have known my dear friend Graham Ettridge for some 33 years. I can honestly say that Graham's generosity and willingness knows no bounds. Since I lost my driving licence on medical grounds 18 months ago, when possible Graham picks me up and drives me to Blunsdon House Hotel Fitness Club weekly for a swim, sauna, steam and jacuzzi and of course a drink and chat in the bar. Graham, using his graphics expertise, designed and produced the cover for my book. As he had already knowledge regarding Amazon publishing, he gave much advice in preparing the book to both myself and Iris, my very patient editor, a lot of support and assistance. In fact Graham gave the book a final proofread prior to actually doing all the uploading onto Amazon for sale in soft and hard cover as well as ebooks for buying and downloading.

Thank you also to the following members of the RAF Masirah & Salalah Old Comrades website who provided me with invaluable information and/or photos that reminded me or added to my knowledge of all things Masirah or associated with Masirah:

Bruce Moyes, Eddie Goodwin, Gerry Rickards, Michael Daley, John Brendan Brown, Colin Blakelock Pomeroy, John Baxter, Ray Flint, John Munro Sneddon, William Cram, David Black, Kevin Patience, Charley Tooley, Geoff Wilson and many others.

As an information source or for checking and confirming information I am grateful to Wikimedia.

PHOTO INDEX

67 SS Baron Innerdale Monument - Author
68 Two ATC Airmen at Monument - Author
69 2014 Masirah Veterans' Re-visit to the Island - Picture courtesy of William Cram
70 Hotel Complex now on Masirah - Public domain
71 Masirah Beach - Author
72 Lookouts from Jetty and Airmen go Sea Swimming - Author
73 1964 High Diving Masirah Style - Photo courtesy of John Sneddon
74 Nosey Crab - Author
75 Loggerhead Turtle Crawls up the Beach - Author
76 Loggerhead Turtle Digs a Hole to Lay Eggs - Author
77 Loggerhead Turtle Lays Eggs - Author
78 Green Turtle - Author
79 Hawksbill Turtle - Wikipedia
80 Olive Ridley Turtle - Wikipedia
81 Baby Turtles Head into the Sea - Author
82 Baby Turtle - Author
83 Author Climbs Hill - Author
84 Lizard - Author
85 Masirah's Rugged Terrain - Author
86 Bondu Bashing in Land Rover - Author
87 World Jury on Reef - Author
88 HMS Llandaff - Wikipedia
89 Old Catalina Base - Author
90 Greenery as we Approach Wadi - Author
91 Villagers - Photo courtesy of Charley Toohey
92 Desalination Plant - Author
93 Swimming Pool - Author
94 A Bluey - Author
95 AOC's Andover - Author
96 Scalextric Kit - Public domain
97 21st Birthday Party - Author
98 Well Tanned Guests - Author
99 Tinnie Stacking – Author

100 Another Busy Day - Author
101 Fred and the Author - Author

[102] Air Traffic Control Tower - Author
[103] Water Bowser - Author
[104] Canberra PR9 - RAF source in public domain
[105] Buccaneer - Author
[106] RAF Buccaneers and their support C130s - Author
[107] Victor Tanker Refuelling a Lightning - RAF source in public domain
[108] Prepositioned Victor Tankers - Author
[109] Vulcan taking off - Author
[110] Royal Navy Wasp Helicopter - Royal Navy source in public domain
[111] Andover Landing Lights - Author
[112] French Navy Elize Anti-Submarine Aircraft - Wikipedia
[113] Kuwait Airways Trident - Public domain
[114] SOAF Strikemaster - Wikipedia
[115] The Standard of the Sultan of Oman - Wikipedia
[116] Shackleton - Author
[117] Hawker Hunter FGA9s - Author
[118] Strikemaster Mk 82 - Author
[119] Percival P56 Piston Provost - Source SOAF in public domain
[120] DHC-2 Beaver - Source SOAF in public domain
[121] SOAF Beaver - Source SOAF in public domain
[122] SOAF C47 - Source SOAF in public domain
[123] Salalah Deterrent - Author
[124] No Nookie Tie - Author
[125] The Logo - Author
[126] 10 Squadron VC10 - RAF source in public domain
[127] Farewell Bahrain - Author
[128] Our Wedding Day - Author
[129] A Memory of Masirah - Author
[130] Queen's Award for Voluntary Service - Author
[131] The Queen at Garden Party - Photo taken by Daphne Logan
[132] Parkinson's Gold Pin - Author
[133] Pride of Swindon Award - Author

Printed in Great Britain
by Amazon

33625567R00116